SECO

ALL ABOUT THE USA 4

A Cultural Reader

Milada Broukal
Janet Milhomme

PEARSON
Longman

D0207197

All About the USA 4: A Cultural Reader, Second Edition

Pearson Education, 10 Bank Street, White Plains, NY 10606

Staff credits: The people who made up the *All About the USA 4* team, representing editorial, production, design, and manufacturing, are: Wendy Campbell, Nan Clarke, Dave Dickey, Melissa Leyva, Robert Ruvo, Paula Van Ells and Pat Wosczyk

Photo credits: p.1 (first) © Car Culture/Corbis, (second) © SuperStock, Inc./SuperStock, (third) egd/Shutterstock; **p.9** © Franz Marc Frei/Corbis; **p.17** © Alex Grimm/Reuters/Corbis; **p.24** William F. Campbell/Getty Images; **p.32** Barbara Jablonska/Shutterstock; **p.46** © Rufus F. Folkks/Corbis; **p.54** (first) Comstock, PictureQuest, (second) Gabriel Moisa/Shutterstock; **p.61** © Bettmann/Corbis; **p.68** © Courtesy of The Library of Congress/Geography and Map Division; **p.75** (first) Galina Barskaya/Shutterstock, (second) Sean Nel/Shutterstock, (third) Ronon/Shutterstock; **p.83** The Metropolitan Museum of Art, Alfred Stieglitz Collection, 1952 (52.203) Image © The Metropolitan Museum of Art; **p.90** (first) © Bettmann/Corbis, (second) Steve Diddle/iStockphoto, (third) © Stuart Westmorland/Corbis; **p.98** (first) Jerry Moorman/iStockphoto, (second) Roman Krochuk/iStockphoto, (third) Patrik Kiefer/iStockphoto; **p.105** © Paul A. Souders/Corbis; **p.112** © Corbis Sygma; **p.119** (first) © Bettmann/Corbis, (second) Jose Antonio Santiso Fernandez/iStockphoto; **p.126** (first) Disney/Pixar/The Kobal Collection, (second) Disney/Pixar/The Kobal Collection, (third) Pixar/Disney/The Kobal Collection; **p.134** © Kim Kulish/Corbis; **p.142** © Bettmann/Corbis; **p.150** Michael Ochs Archives/Getty Images; **p.157** Lucas Film/20th Century Fox/The Kobal Collection; **p.164** Lambert/Getty Images; **p.172** (first) © Michael Ochs Archives/Corbis, (second) © Neal Preston/Corbis, (third) Mike Powell/Getty Images

Text composition: Integra
Text font: 11.5/15 New Aster

Library of Congress Cataloging-in-Publication Data
Broukal, Milada.
  All about the USA / Milada Broukal.— 2nd ed.
      p. cm.
  Rev. ed. of: All about the USA, 1st ed. 1999.
  Revised ed. will be published in 4 separate volume levels.
  ISBN 0-13-613892-6 (student bk. with audio cd v. 1,: alk. paper)
  ISBN 0-13-240628-4 (student bk. with audio cd v. 2,: alk. paper)
  ISBN 0-13-234969-8 (student bk. with audio cd v. 3,: alk. paper)
  ISBN 0-13-234968-X (student bk. with audio cd v. 4,: alk. paper)
  1. Readers—United States.   2. English language—Textbooks for foreign
speakers.   3. United States—Civilization—Problems, exercises, etc.
I. Murphy, Peter (Peter Lewis Keane), 1947-   II. Milhomme, Janet.
III. Title.
  PE1127.H5B68 2008
  428.64—dc22
                                                              2007032614

ISBN-10: 0-13-234968-X
ISBN-13: 978-0-13-234968-0

Printed in the United States of America
2 3 4 5 6 7 8 9 10—CRK—12 11 10 09 08

CONTENTS

INTRODUCTION

All About the USA 4 is a high-intermediate reader for students of English as a Second Language. Twenty-four units introduce typically American people, places, and things. A host of facts presented in the units will not only provide students with information about the USA, but will also stimulate cross-cultural exchange. The vocabulary and structures used in the text have been carefully controlled at a high- intermediate level, while every effort has been made to keep the language natural.

Each unit contains:
- Prereading questions and introductory visuals
- A reading passage (650—950 words, with progressing level of difficulty)
- Topic-related vocabulary work
- Skimming for main ideas
- Scanning for details
- Making Inferences and Concluding
- Discussion questions
- A writing assignment
- Research and Presentation assignments

The **PREREADING** questions are linked to the visual on the first page of each unit. They focus the student on the topic of the unit by introducing names, encouraging speculation about content, involving the students' own experience when possible, and presenting vocabulary as the need arises.

The **READING** of each passage should, ideally, first be done individually by skimming for a general feel for the content. The teacher may wish to deal with some of the vocabulary at this point. A second, more detailed individual reading could be done while working through the vocabulary Meaning exercise. Further reading(s) could be done aloud with the teacher or with the class.

The two **VOCABULARY** exercises focus on the bolded words in the reading. Meaning, a definition exercise, encourages students to work out the meanings from the context. Within this group are groups of words or collocations that are easier to learn together the way they are used in the language. The second exercise, Use, reinforces the vocabulary further by providing students with the opportunity to use the words in a meaningful, yet possibly different, context. This section can be done during or after the reading phase, or both.

There are four **COMPREHENSION** exercises. *Skimming for Main Ideas* should be used in conjunction with the text to help students develop their reading skills, and not as a test of memory. In each case, the students are asked to confirm the basic content of the text, which they can do either individually, or in pairs, in small groups, or as a whole class. *Scanning for Details* concentrates on the scanning skills necessary to derive maximum value from reading. *Ordering Events* concentrates on developing a sense of the organization of the reading and develops the skill of spatial organization. *Making Inferences and Concluding* develops the skill of inferring meaning from what is not directly stated in the passage by "reading between the lines."

DISCUSSION gives the students the opportunity to bring their own knowledge and imagination to the topics and related areas. They may wish to discuss all of the questions in their small groups or select one on which to report back to the class.

WRITING provides stimulus for students to express their own ideas by writing one or more short paragraphs related to the topic of the reading. Teachers should use their own judgment when deciding whether to correct the writing exercises.

RESEARCH AND PRESENTATION continues and expands the theme of the unit by providing students with the opportunity to do research and then develop and deliver a presentation to the class based on their research findings.

Additional Assignment Suggestions:

A Summary: This oral or written exercise focuses attention on expressing the main ideas of the passage in the students' own words. Students can retell the reading passage or write a one-paragraph summary of it, focusing on the key points and making sure that all the main points are discussed. Students may not copy from the reading.

Restatement: This exercise allows students to practice newly learned vocabulary in a clearly constructed paragraph. After choosing a particular paragraph from the passage, students read it several times and then restate the content in their own words. This exercise can also be done orally.

Cars in America

PREREADING

Answer the questions.

1. Do you own a car? If so, what kind is it?
2. What is your favorite car? Why?
3. Do you like to travel by car? Why?

Cars in America

1   Driving in the 1890s was an adventure. The first cars in America rode on rough dirt roads. They made **clouds of dust**. Most of the cars had no **windshields** and no tops. Riders had no protection from the dust and dirt. There were also insects and sudden rain showers. Even on a nice day, a driver was sure to have **a flat tire** or a breakdown. There were no repair shops or emergency services. Motorists had to make repairs themselves on the side of the road.

2   There were other problems, too. Cars had no lights and no horns. They had bad brakes and a difficult steering system. They also had too many levers to make the car go faster and slower. Drivers often became confused. Cars went out of control, and accidents were common. People, animals, and horse-drawn carts were all in danger from the new vehicles on the road. The new drivers were pretty dangerous, too! However, none of this made people love the auto any less. In fact by 1900, most upper-class Americans owned one. Automobiles were a symbol of wealth and sophistication.*

3   A man named Henry Ford wanted to make a car that was affordable** for everyone. He made the Model T. It sold for $850. It was so popular that Ford couldn't keep up with demand. Americans were falling in love with the automobile. That love changed America forever.

4   America was a big country. Long distances separated people and cities. The car gave Americans a new freedom. As years passed, cars and roads improved. More and more Americans bought cars and began to drive. The Sunday drive became a popular weekend activity. Families packed a picnic lunch. People who lived in rural areas—places in the countryside—traveled to the city. People who lived in the city traveled to the country. New businesses were built along the roads. There were filling stations where drivers got gas and roadside **diners** where people stopped to eat. Shops opened that sold gifts and maps. After a while, new communities began to appear along popular routes.

5   In 1924, the first drive-in restaurant was built in Florida. Motorists parked outside. Someone came out to take and deliver orders. People ate in their cars. Drive-in restaurants spread across the country. People loved them!

6   The next year, the world's first motel was built in California. The owner made up the word. It meant motor hotel. Guests paid $1.25 a night to stay in a two-room cottage with a kitchen. The cottages*** were built around a **courtyard** with a swimming pool. Like the drive-in restaurant,

---

sophistication: a combination of wisdom, confidence, and culture in a person
**affordable*: something that people have enough money to buy
***cottages*: small houses with only two or three rooms

the motel was a big success. Soon, motels were built along roads around the country. People started driving longer distances and staying overnight. Business owners liked to travel in the summertime. After a while, they gave their workers time off, too. The summer vacation was born. In June, July, and August, the roads were full of cars. People were driving to the beach, parks, and other places of interest.

7   Another popular invention was the drive-in movie. People went to the drive-in in the evening. They paid someone and then drove into a huge parking lot and parked near a **speaker**. They sat in their cars and watched a movie on a huge outdoor screen. In the 1940s, drive-ins began to spread across the country. They were very popular. They increased from 1,000 in 1948 to close to 5,000 by 1958.

8   By the 1950s, automobiles had changed the American way of life. People no longer had to live in cities in order to work. They could drive to their jobs. Country towns began to grow rapidly. City areas **expanded** into places that had been empty before. These areas became known as the suburbs. Soon shopping centers were built near the new suburbs. By then, almost every family had a car. They used it to go everywhere. Cars were faster, better, and more beautiful than ever. There were big family cars that held eight people. Sports cars were popular with young drivers. The American car culture was **at its height**. Cars were celebrated in books, songs, and movies. There were roads and highways all across the country. People loved to drive around the country and see America. Nothing symbolized American independence and personal freedom like the car.

9   As the **decades** passed, the American population increased and so did the number of cars on the road. Families no longer had one car. They had one for every member of driving age. Soon the roads became **clogged** with traffic. More roads were built, but they were not just highways with two lanes. They were superhighways with four, six, and even eight lanes on each side. Soon they were full of cars, too. The air in cities became polluted from so many trucks, buses, and autos. Gas prices went up and up. Yet Americans continued to drive, one to a car, day after day.

10   Americans still love their cars. But today they realize that their cars are also part of a big problem. They lose hundreds of hours a year sitting in traffic. They are getting sick from the air pollution. They are paying more money for fuel. Americans are starting to think about buying cars that use cleaner fuel. They are asking for more public transportation. They are thinking about the future. Only time will tell if one day Americans will look back and see their car culture as simply a part of the nation's colorful history.

VOCABULARY

 MEANING

Complete each definition with one of the following. Guess your answers, and then check them with a dictionary.

clouds of dust	a flat tire	courtyard	expanded	decades
windshields	diners	speaker	at its height	clogged

1. If something is _____, it has material filling up a space, causing it to be blocked so it cannot work or flow properly.

2. If you have _____, the air has gone out of your tire and it will not roll.

3. Something that has _____ has grown larger.

4. _____ happen when something causes the air to be full of tiny pieces of earth, like dust, floating around in an area.

5. _____ are pieces of glass in the front part of cars that drivers look through.

6. _____ are periods of ten years.

7. A _____ is a part of something, such as a radio, that produces sound so others can hear what is being said or played.

8. An outdoor space that has walls or buildings around it is a _____.

9. Small restaurants beside the road are _____.

10. When something is _____, it is at its greatest point of use, success, or interest.

 USE

Work with a partner to answer the questions. Use complete sentences.

1. What are some things that stop working when they are *clogged*?
2. What is a fashion that is no longer *at its height*?
3. What are some things that can get *a flat tire*?
4. What is something that has a *speaker*?
5. What can send *clouds of dust* into an area?
6. What are some things that have *windshields*?

7. What kind of food is usually served at *diners*?

8. What city in your country has *expanded* greatly in the last fifty years?

COMPREHENSION

 SKIMMING FOR MAIN IDEAS

Quickly read to find the main idea of each paragraph, and then circle the letter of the best answer.

1. Paragraph 2 is mainly about
   a. problems having to do with the first cars.
   b. the accidents people had in the first cars.
   c. the importance of cars as a symbol of wealth.

2. The main topic of paragraph 6 is
   a. what the world's first motel looked like.
   b. what people did while they were on vacation.
   c. how the first motels changed people's habits.

3. The main topic of paragraph 8 is that
   a. cars were changed and improved over the years.
   b. people loved cars so much that they wrote about them and made music and movies.
   c. cars changed where and how people lived.

4. The last paragraph is mainly about how Americans are
   a. starting to buy cars that pollute the air less.
   b. realizing the problems that cars are causing.
   c. asking for more public transportation.

 SCANNING FOR DETAILS

Reread the passage quickly to find key words and phrases from the questions. Then circle the letter of the correct answer.

1. When a car broke down, it was difficult for a driver in the 1890s because there were no
   a. other drivers on the road.
   b. extra parts or tires.
   c. places that repaired cars.

2. The first cars had no
   a. steering system.
   b. lights.
   c. brakes.

3. The Model T was extremely popular because it
   a. was safe.
   b. was not very expensive.
   c. had a better engine than other cars.

4. In the early days of car ownership, people loved to go driving on
   a. weekdays.
   b. evenings.
   c. weekends.

5. Early drivers got gas at
   a. filling stations.
   b. diners.
   c. gift shops.

6. The first drive-in restaurant was built in
   a. Florida.
   b. California.
   c. New York.

7. Once motels were built, people were able to
   a. get their cars fixed.
   b. stop to eat while they were on the road.
   c. drive longer distances.

8. People went to the drive-in
   a. at night.
   b. in the afternoon.
   c. early in the morning.

9. Cars made it possible for people to live in the suburbs because
   a. they could stay overnight in the city.
   b. they could drive to work.
   c. they could go shopping near their homes.

10. To help solve traffic problems today, Americans are asking for
    a. more public transportation.
    b. wider roads.
    c. bigger cars.

⭐ ORDERING EVENTS

Number the sentences to show the correct order. Do this without looking at the passage. Then reread the passage to check your answers.

_____ People begin to move to areas outside of the cities.

_____ The first drive-in restaurant is built.

_____ Most upper-class Americans own cars.

_____ People begin to enjoy trips to places outside their home areas as roads  and cars improve.

_____ Highways and superhighways cannot hold all of the cars.

_____ Henry Ford makes the Model T.

_____ Americans begin to question their car culture.

MAKING INFERENCES AND CONCLUDING

Information is not always stated directly in a passage. Sometimes we make guesses—inferences or conclusions—from the information that is in the reading. The answers to these questions are not directly stated in the passage. Circle the letter of the best answer.

1. From the passage, we can conclude that
   a. the first cars were dangerous, troublesome, and difficult to drive.
   b. the first drivers were trained well before they started to drive.
   c. problems with the first cars stopped people from liking and buying them.

2. We can infer from the passage that automobiles
   a. played a big part in the growth of new businesses.
   b. caused problems between workers and business owners.
   c. became less important as people moved to the suburbs.

3. The writer seems to say that
   a. Americans' love of cars comes only from their necessity to drive long distances.
   b. Americans will never make the changes necessary to stop the harm done by owning so many cars.
   c. cars have always meant more to Americans than just a means of transportation.

DISCUSSION

Discuss the answers to the questions with your classmates.

1. Do you think that the type of car people drive says something about them? Why? What are some cars that are especially symbolic? What other things do people own that say something about who they are?

2. What made Americans need, want, and love cars more than people in other countries?

3. What company do you think makes the best automobiles? Why?

4. What are some steps that can be taken to reduce the effects of car pollution around the world?

WRITING

The invention of the automobile helped people everywhere to live better lives, but it also caused problems. Write one or more paragraphs about the advantages and disadvantages of the invention of the automobile. Be sure to give specific examples to support your opinions.

RESEARCH AND PRESENTATION

Find out what company produces each of these models of cars and where their headquarters are located. Get information about what type of car it is (luxury, sport, racing, hybrid), what the average cost is, and what type of customer, in general, buys it.

1. BMW E39 M5 Touring
2. Cadillac Deville
3. Corvette
4. Kia
5. Lamborghini
6. Land Rover
7. Prius (Toyota)
8. Rolls Royce Phantom

Now work with a partner or small group. Make a poster with a picture for one of the cars and present it to your class. Give all the necessary information a person needs in order to buy one. Be prepared to answer questions.

DID YOU KNOW . . . ?

On the widest road in the world, the Monumental Axis in Brazil, 160 cars can drive side by side.

The Building of the Brooklyn Bridge

PREREADING

Answer the questions.

1. Where are bridges built? What purpose do bridges serve?

2. What are some different kinds of bridges?

3. What is the most famous bridge in your country? Where is it?

The Building of the Brooklyn Bridge

1. In the early 1800s, the only way to travel from Brooklyn to Manhattan was by ferry across the East River. Sometimes the trip was pleasant, but more often it was uncomfortable and dangerous. In winter, ice blocks sometimes made the trip impossible. In 1852, John Roebling announced that he wanted to build a bridge across the river.

2. Ferryboat operators didn't want a bridge. Others said it was impossible. For years, Roebling tried to **convince** people that he could build the bridge they needed. In the winter of 1867, the East River froze. People were stuck in Brooklyn. No one could get to work in Manhattan, or to theaters, restaurants, and places they enjoyed. People were unhappy and finally asked Roebling to build a bridge.

3. Roebling was born in 1806 in a German village. His father owned a tobacco shop. He wanted his son to work with him, but Roebling studied engineering. He was **fascinated with** bridges. In 1831, he moved to America and worked on canal equipment. He invented wire cable to use instead of ropes to pull ships through canals. Then he got the idea that suspension bridges could be made stronger by using iron cable rather than ropes and **chains**.

4. A suspension bridge is different from other bridges because the roadway hangs in the air, **suspended** from thick cables. On most bridges, the roadway is built on many **supports**. There isn't much room for boats to pass between them, and they can't be built high enough for the tallest boats. With a suspension bridge, two high towers that can be built far apart hold the cables, so boats can use the river. In 1846, Roebling built a suspension bridge over the Monongahela River, followed by bridges over Niagara Falls and the Cincinnati River.

5. Building a suspension bridge over the East River presented problems. The river was deep and moved fast. There were strong winds and heavy boat traffic. The bridge had to be high enough so the tallest ships could pass underneath it. The biggest problem was the length of the bridge because the East River was half a mile wide. The suspension bridge would have to be the longest ever built.

6. In June of 1869, John Roebling finished his design. He and his son Washington went to the Fulton Ferry Pier in Brooklyn to examine the work area. John **was concentrating** so hard that he didn't see a ferry coming toward him. His son called out, but it was too late. The boat hit where John was standing and **crushed** his foot. The injury soon **became infected**, and John Roebling died a month later.

7. Washington Roebling decided to continue John's work and became chief engineer of the Brooklyn Bridge. Washington had a huge job ahead of him. First he had to build underwater foundations to support the two

enormous bridge towers. Because the river bottom was sand and mud, he had to dig through to the solid rock at least 40 feet below. He designed two gigantic wooden boxes called caissons. First, the wood was made waterproof. The caisson was then put on the bottom of the river. It rose above the water, and workers climbed inside and went down tall ladders. Inside, 100 workers dug out dirt and rocks with simple hand tools. As they removed the dirt, the caisson sank into the mud. At the same time, workers were building the tower on top of the caisson. The weight of the tower pushed it farther into the mud until it reached solid rock. One caisson took months to build.

8   The men in the caissons were in constant danger. Many got "caisson disease," or what is today called "the bends." At the river bottom, the weight of the water against the caisson made the air **pressure** inside rise. As the men climbed the ladders from the high pressure at the bottom to normal pressure at the top, their bodies needed time to **adjust to** the pressure change. They didn't know they had to come up slowly. Many suffered terrible pains, some were paralyzed, and others died. Caisson disease almost killed Washington, too. He couldn't walk or talk and had to stay home in bed.

9   Washington used binoculars* to watch the construction from the bedroom window of his house above the East River. His wife, Emily, took directions to the workers. She was very intelligent and had learned about suspension bridges from John and Washington, so she started making decisions on her own. At first, the men didn't want to work with her because she was a woman, but eventually Emily earned their respect.

10   When the towers were finished, huge steel cables were strung between them. The Roeblings used steel instead of iron because steel is stronger. Each cable was made of over 3,500 miles of steel wire bound together. After the cables were completed, the road was built. In 1883, the bridge was finished. Twenty-one men had lost their lives because of sickness or accidents.

11   On May 24, 1883, the Brooklyn Bridge was opened. It was beautiful, graceful, and elegant. President Chester A. Arthur walked across the bridge from New York to meet Emily on the other side. That night there were fireworks. Hundreds of thousands of people celebrated. Washington and Emily watched from their bedroom window. After 14 years, their work was finished.

---

*binoculars: a specially made pair of glasses that is used for looking at distant objects

VOCABULARY

⭐ MEANING

What is the meaning of the underlined words? Circle the letter of the correct answer. Use a dictionary to check your answers.

1. Roebling tried to <u>convince</u> people that he could build a bridge.
   a. cause someone to believe
   b. take complete control over someone
   c. make someone confused

2. Roebling was <u>fascinated with</u> bridges.
   a. bored with
   b. frightened of
   c. interested in

3. Iron cable was stronger than <u>chains</u>.
   a. large ropes twisted together
   b. metal rings connected together
   c. many wires bound together

4. On suspension bridges, the roadways are <u>suspended</u> from cables.
   a. attached to
   b. made
   c. hung

5. Most bridges have roadways that are built on <u>supports</u>.
   a. things that hold the weight of something else
   b. things that rise above something else
   c. things that make something else stronger

6. Before his accident, John Roebling <u>was concentrating</u> very hard on his work.
   a. was keeping his thoughts on
   b. was trying to decide on
   c. was dreaming about

7. John's foot was <u>crushed</u> in the accident.
   a. moved aside quickly
   b. pressed with great force
   c. cut very deeply

8. His injury <u>became infected</u>.
   a. swelled up
   b. got diseased
   c. came to be better

9. The water made the air <u>pressure</u> rise inside the caisson.
   a. force or weight of
   b. movement of
   c. temperature of

10. The workers needed time for their bodies to <u>adjust to</u> the pressure change.
    a. endure, or put up with
    b. remove by force
    c. make right or correct

USE

Work with a partner to answer the questions. Use complete sentences.

1. What are some objects that have *supports*?
2. What are some different uses for *chains*?
3. What person or thing are you *fascinated with*?
4. What is a way to *convince* someone to change his or her mind?
5. How do changes in air *pressure* affect climbers as they climb higher up a mountain?
6. What are some things that are *suspended* from ropes, chains, or cables?
7. What happens to an object when it is *crushed*?
8. What are some changes that travelers often have to *adjust to*?

COMPREHENSION

 SKIMMING FOR MAIN IDEAS

Quickly read to find the main idea of each paragraph, and then circle the letter of the best answer.

1. Paragraph 1 is mainly about
   a. transportation in the 1800s.
   b. the difficulties of ferry travel.
   c. John Roebling's desire to build a bridge.

2. The main topic of paragraph 3 is
   a. John Roebling's early life and his accomplishments.
   b. John Roebling's childhood.
   c. John Roebling's move to America.

3. The main topic of paragraph 5 is
   a. the difficulties of building a bridge over the East River.
   b. why John Roebling wanted to build a suspension bridge over the East River.
   c. how the East River was used by the people of Brooklyn.

4. Paragraph 7 is mainly about
   a. the type of labor the workers had to do.
   b. the underwater conditions of the East River.
   c. the building of the underwater foundations.

 SCANNING FOR DETAILS

Reread the passage quickly to find key words and phrases from the questions. Then write the correct answer on the line.

1. People in Brooklyn asked John Roebling to build a bridge after _____ in the winter.
2. John Roebling's father wanted him to _____.
3. Roebling had to build a bridge that was high enough for _____.
4. _____ hold the cables on a suspension bridge.
5. Washington Roebling couldn't build the foundations on the river bottom because _____.
6. The workers in the caisson used simple hand tools to _____.
7. The air pressure was high at the bottom of the caisson because of _____.
8. The bridge workers didn't want to work with Emily Roebling at first because _____.
9. Once the towers were finished, the next job was to _____.
10. It took _____ years to make the Brooklyn Bridge.

 ORDERING EVENTS

Number the sentences to show the correct order. Do this without looking at the passage. Then reread the passage to check your answers.

_____ People asked Roebling to build them a bridge over the East River.

_____ Washington Roebling built two huge caissons.

_____ Emily Roebling took control of the building of the Brooklyn Bridge.

_____ John Roebling built a bridge over Niagara Falls.

_____ John Roebling was hurt in an accident.

_____ People couldn't get to work in Manhattan.

_____ Washington Roebling nearly died from caisson disease.

MAKING INFERENCES AND CONCLUDING

Information is not always stated directly in a passage. Sometimes we make guesses—inferences or conclusions—from the information that is in the reading. The answers to these questions are not directly stated in the passage. Circle the letter of the best answer.

1. From the passage, we can conclude that
   a. many people in Brooklyn were disappointed with the bridge.
   b. some people were against the bridge because it hurt their business.
   c. most people didn't need a bridge across the East River.

2. The writer seems to say that
   a. most of the bridge workers worked under safe conditions.
   b. most of the workers knew how to avoid caisson disease.
   c. building the bridge was dangerous for everyone involved.

3. We can infer from the passage that
   a. the Roeblings made many sacrifices to build the bridge.
   b. Emily Roebling could never get the workers to do what she wanted.
   c. The Roeblings were never appreciated for the work they did on the Brooklyn Bridge.

DISCUSSION

Discuss the answers to the questions with your classmates.

1. What are some important bridges, buildings, and other structures in your country? Where are they located? What makes them important?
2. What are some jobs that are dangerous?
3. Why do you think people do dangerous work?
4. How has safety in the workplace changed over the years? Are working conditions in most jobs better today than many years ago?

WRITING

Write one or more paragraphs about a famous structure (bridge, building, dam, castle, or other construction) that you think is the most beautiful or impressive in the world. First, describe it in detail. Then explain why you like it and why you think it is important.

RESEARCH AND PRESENTATION

Below is a list of famous structures in America. Find out where each one is located, some of its important features, and why it is famous.

1. Empire State Building
2. Gateway Arch
3. Golden Gate Bridge
4. Hoover Dam
5. Sears Tower
6. Space Needle
7. Statue of Liberty
8. Washington Monument

Now work with a partner or small group. Make a poster, and prepare a presentation with photos about one of the structures for the class. Be prepared to answer questions.

DID YOU KNOW . . . ?

There are approximately 600,000 rivets (special nails) in each of the two towers of the Golden Gate Bridge over the San Francisco Bay. That's more than 1 million rivets!

Yo-Yo Ma

PREREADING

Answer the questions.

1. Do you like classical music? Why?
2. Who is a famous classical musician in your country?
3. Who were some famous composers of classical music?

Yo-Yo Ma

1   People **leaned forward** in their chairs. The music they were listening to was beautiful. "He's a genius," they whispered. When the concert ended, the musician smiled and took a bow.* His parents looked at him proudly. Their five-year-old son, Yo-Yo Ma, had performed well. Perhaps they already guessed that he would become one of the world's most famous cellists.

2   Yo-Yo Ma was born in Paris on October 7, 1955, to Chinese parents. His father wrote music. His mother was a singer and musician. At a very early age, Ma eagerly studied the violin and piano. At age four he began to study the cello, a musical instrument with four strings. The cello is part of the violin family, but it is larger than a violin and makes a deeper sound. Ma learned the cello quickly. When he was five years old, he was giving concerts. He played as well as an adult. He was what people call a child prodigy.

3   Ma's family moved to New York when he was seven years old. At the age of eight he appeared on American television. He played in a concert conducted by the famous Leonard Bernstein. Ma was a good and obedient boy at home, but he was a different boy at school. He was **rebellious** and got into trouble. His teachers finally realized that Ma was bored with his schoolwork. He was **way ahead** of his classmates. The teachers put him into advanced classes. At age fifteen he graduated from high school.

4   Ma attended the Juilliard School of Music, a famous school known around the world. He was performing many recitals during this time and making some money. He knew he could make a living as a musician. He enrolled in Columbia University, but then he **dropped out**. He went against his parent's wishes. Eventually he enrolled at Harvard. Again he wanted to drop out, but his parents said that he must complete his education. Ma graduated from Harvard.

5   Soon Ma was getting famous. He performed with many of the world's major orchestras. He made recordings and played with other famous musicians. As the years went by, his work became known to the world. Ma became one of the world's most famous and most favorite cellists. But Ma never let celebrity** change him or his music.

6   Ma feels deeply that music should not just entertain. He believes it should **touch the hearts** of people and bring them closer together. He believes that music has a message for people. The message comes through him and his instrument to his audience. Ma uses his music to connect people to him and to each other. Ma does not play only classical music. He is very **versatile**. He is inspired by other artists and their music. He

---

took a bow: bent forward from the waist to show respect and accept praise
**celebrity*: fame or popularity

likes to blend many kinds of music into his performances. He has played tango music from Argentina and traditional Chinese melodies. He has also played with African musicians, traditional American bluegrass musicians, and many others. He has made **soundtracks** for movies. He has even performed for the Muppets puppets on the *Sesame Street* television show!

7   Ma is a man with **exceptional** talent, but he is also a humble person. He helps others in many ways. He will do any task when he is needed. Once he left his $2.5 million, 300-year-old cello in a New York City taxicab. Fortunately, he got it back unharmed. After that he recorded a message that was played in New York City taxis. The message reminded passengers to take their belongings with them. Ma laughed at himself for being so forgetful. Ma loves to spend time with his family. Every July he takes the month off to be with them. In 1977, he married Jill Horner, a violinist. They have two children, Nicholas and Emily. Ma's older sister, Yeou-Cheng Ma, is also a violinist. Her husband is a guitarist. Together the family runs the Children's Orchestra Society in Long Island, New York.

8   Ma is very happy playing music. He believes it is his destiny. But like everyone, Ma has had some hard times in his life. In 1980, he found out that he had scoliosis, a condition where the spine is curved. Ma thought his career was over, and he was very unhappy. Finally he decided to have an operation. It was a success. Ma learned from his hardship. He learned to enjoy the things he was given. He learned to always make the best of things.

9   Yo-Yo Ma currently has an organization called Silk Road. He believes that music is a **universal** language that brings people together. Silk Road brings together composers and musicians from ten different countries around the world. They write and play both traditional and classical music. Ma plays with Silk Road. He also continues to give his own performances in concert halls and many other places. With his moving and **inspirational** music, he brings joy to people around the world.

VOCABULARY

MEANING

Complete each definition with one of the following. Guess your answers, and then check them with a dictionary.

leaned forward	way ahead	touch the hearts	soundtracks	universal
rebellious	dropped out	versatile	exceptional	inspirational

1. _____ are recorded music for movies.

2. If you _____, you moved your body toward what was in front of you.

3. If a person can do many things, he or she is _____.

4. A person who stopped attending or participating in courses and other activities _____ of a school or organization.

5. Something is _____ if it causes you to have creative feelings or ideas that you didn't have before.

6. To be _____ is to be farther along, to know more or have more ability.

7. A _____ person goes against the rules.

8. Something _____ is unusual in a good way.

9. To _____ of people is to cause them to feel deep emotion.

10. Something that everyone can understand or experience is _____.

USE

Work with a partner to answer the questions. Use complete sentences.

1. If a person *leaned forward* too far, what might happen?
2. Who is someone you know with *exceptional* talent?
3. What are some needs that are *universal* among people?
4. What kinds of song *touch the hearts* of people?
5. Who is a famous performer who is very *versatile*?
6. What are some ways in which teenagers are *rebellious*?
7. What book, song, or person has been *inspirational* for you?
8. What is your favorite *soundtrack* from a movie?

COMPREHENSION

SKIMMING FOR MAIN IDEAS

Quickly read to find the main idea of each paragraph, and then circle the letter of the best answer.

1. Paragraph 1 is mainly about
   a. how Yo-Yo Ma's parents believed he would someday be famous.
   b. how people reacted to Ma's childhood performances.
   c. how Yo-Yo Ma behaved as a child musician.

2. The main topic of paragraph 4 is
   a. Yo-Yo Ma's development as a musician.
   b. the history of Ma's formal education.
   c. Yo-Yo Ma's relationship with his parents.

3. The main topic of paragraph 5 is
   a. Yo-Yo Ma's many skills as a musician.
   b. Yo-Yo Ma's beliefs and interests concerning music.
   c. Yo-Yo Ma's experiences as a musician.

4. Paragraph 8 is mainly about
   a. how Ma feels when he's playing music.
   b. how Ma suffered with scoliosis.
   c. how having scoliosis affected Ma.

SCANNING FOR DETAILS

Reread the passage quickly to find key words and phrases from the questions. Each sentence has an incorrect fact. Cross out the incorrect fact, and write the correct answer above it.

1. Yo-Yo Ma was born in London in 1955 to Chinese parents.

2. Both of Ma's parents were doctors.

3. A cello is a three-stringed musical instrument.

4. When Ma was seven, he appeared on American television.

5. Yo-Yo Ma graduated from Columbia University.

6. Yo-Yo Ma likes to play tango music from Africa.

7. After Ma left his cello in a taxi, he recorded a message that told people not to take taxis in New York.

8. Yo-Yo Ma and other family members run the Children's Orchestra Society in Los Angeles.

9. Scoliosis is a disease that affects a person's legs.

10. Silk Road brings together musicians from Europe and America.

 ## ORDERING EVENTS

Number the sentences to show the correct order. Do this without looking at the passage. Then reread the passage to check your answers.

_____ Yo-Yo Ma attended the Juilliard School of Music.

_____ Ma's family moved to New York.

_____ Ma organized Silk Road.

_____ Ma graduated from Harvard.

_____ Yo-Yo Ma became world famous.

_____ Ma played in a concert conducted by Leonard Bernstein.

MAKING INFERENCES AND CONCLUDING

Information is not always stated directly in a passage. Sometimes we make guesses—inferences or conclusions—from the information that is in the reading. The answers to these questions are not directly stated in the passage. Circle the letter of the best answer.

1. From the passage, we can conclude that
   a. Yo-Yo Ma's unusual talent made him unhappy as child.
   b. Yo-Yo Ma showed a love as well as ability for music early in life.
   c. Yo-Yo Ma didn't want to learn music, so he went against his parents' wishes.

2. We can infer from the passage that Yo-Yo Ma
   a. is uncomfortable outside the area of classical music.
   b. has never been too proud to learn from others.
   c. is not eager to share his success with others.

3. The writer seems to say that Yo-Yo Ma
   a. believes his music can benefit the world.
   b. finds happiness only in his music.
   c. has allowed his fame and celebrity to interfere with his music.

DISCUSSION

Discuss the answers to the questions with your classmates.

1. Many people admire Yo-Yo Ma. Why do you think this is true? What are his best qualities?
2. How does hardship often help us to become better people?
3. Do you agree with Ma that music is a universal language that can bring people together? Why?
4. If you had an opportunity to learn any musical instrument, which would you choose? Why?

WRITING

Do you think that children who are "prodigies" are as happy as normal children? Write one or more paragraphs that give your opinion and discuss the advantages and disadvantages of being a child prodigy.

RESEARCH AND PRESENTATION

Below is a list of famous musicians. Find out where and when they were born and what they did that made them famous.

1. Louis Armstrong
2. Johannes Brahms
3. Mick Jagger
4. Scott Joplin
5. B. B. King
6. Bob Marley
7. Carlos Santana
8. Igor Stravinsky

Now work with a partner or small group. Develop a short presentation about one of the musicians. Include a photo and a recording of music written or performed by the artist. Be prepared to answer questions.

DID YOU KNOW...?
Wolfgang Mozart learned to play the piano at age five and could write music before he could write words. By age twenty-one, he had completed 300 works of music!

The Spirit of the Wolf

PREREADING

Answer the questions.

1. Are there wolves in your country? If so, where are they found?
2. What stories do you know about a wolf?

The Spirit of the Wolf

1   Long before the first humans found their way to North America, gray wolves lived in almost every part of the continent. When Native Americans lived in these areas, they had great respect for the wolves, as they did for nature and all its creatures. They depended upon animals for food, clothing, and shelter. They also admired animals for their cunning, strength, and **agility**. Newborn babies were often named after an animal, such as Running Deer or Little Eagle. An important chief of the Cheyenne people was named High Backed Wolf. To Native Americans, the wolf was a very special animal.

2   The Native Americans believed that the world was filled with spirits that controlled their lives. All things in nature, such as the sun, the mountains, the snake, eagle, and wolf had a spirit within them. To **honor** the spirits and ask them for help, ceremonies were performed. One of them was the animal dance of the Cheyenne. For this ceremony, there were many special **rites**. One was the painting of a wolf skin in a certain manner. Another was that the men put on skins of various animals, including the wolf, and danced around a special fire. It was believed this ceremony would bring the tribe good fortune when they went out to hunt. It was important to have the spirit of the wolf with them. The natives knew the wolf was a great hunter. They also admired its many other qualities.

3   In the wild, wolves have great strength and **endurance**. Their thick fur protects them from temperatures as low as 50 degrees below zero. They travel in family groups called *packs* and are intelligent, loving, and **loyal**. There are a number of wolf species. In America, the Arctic wolf and the timber wolf are found, as well as the smaller and darker red wolf of Texas and the Mexican wolf. Wolves can adapt to a variety of habitats.*

4   The northern wolf is a very handsome animal that looks like a big, friendly dog. In the far north, it is often white. In the south, it is gray. Wolves are very social animals. They travel, hunt, and perform almost all other activities in the company of other wolves. A pack usually consists of a male and female that will stay together for life and have babies, or pups. They are constant and loving companions. The other members are usually their young, ranging in age from tiny pups to two- and three-year-olds. Most packs include six or seven members but can include as many as fifteen.

5   The parent wolves are the leaders. The rest of the wolves, depending upon their age and strength, all have their own special places. Their relationships are very complicated. Scientific studies have shown that wolf packs have **complex** rules that govern their behavior and the way

---

habitats: the environments in which they live

they relate to each other. Their methods of communicating are also very elaborate. Although wolves make many different kinds of sounds, the most famous is the **howl**. Wolves howl at any time, not just at night. It's a way of sharing their closeness as a group. One wolf will point its nose toward the sky and start to howl. Immediately, the other pack members will rush over and join him. The whole group is excited and happy. Packs also communicate with each other this way. They tell each other to stay out of their territory.

6   In wolf families, everything is done as a group, including the raising of the young. They trust and depend on each other from birth. Probably the most important activity in the life of the pack is hunting. Wolves are carnivorous, or meat eaters. They live on a variety of foods, from mice to fish to the larger deer and moose. Wolves only kill what they can eat. Hunting in packs is necessary for chasing and killing large prey. Wolves never attack a large, healthy deer or moose, which can easily defend itself with sharp kicks. Wolves **pursue** herds to find the sick or weak members. This may seem cruel, but they are actually doing the herd good by keeping it strong. Also, without natural enemies, herds will overpopulate their territory and use up the food supply. Many will eventually starve. Wolves are needed to keep the balance of nature.

7   Unfortunately, the people who settled America did not respect the wolf like the natives did. Over the years, wolves were hunted, poisoned, and destroyed in great numbers. They are now rare in North America. However, many people now believe the wolf has a rightful place among America's wildlife. In some places, like Yellowstone National Park, they have been put back into the wild. There is much **controversy** about this. Ranchers complain that the wolves attack their herds. Hunters also don't like wolves in the wild. They want the deer to overpopulate so they can hunt them. At the same time, there are many people who are fighting to let the wolf once again **roam** freely in the remaining wild lands of America. The argument over putting wolves back into the wild is certain to continue for many years. Only time will tell whether they will one day be allowed to do that, and if the spirit of the wolf will live on.

VOCABULARY

 **MEANING**

What is the meaning of the underlined words? Circle the letter of the correct answer. Use a dictionary to check your answers.

1. Animals are admired for their cunning, strength, and <u>agility</u>.
   a. gentleness
   b. quickness
   c. cautiousness

2. The Native Americans performed ceremonies to <u>honor</u> the spirits.
   a. show respect for
   b. accept
   c. ask favors from

3. For the ceremony, they performed special <u>rites</u>.
   a. rhythmic movements
   b. religious celebrations
   c. fixed ceremonial actions

4. Wolves have great strength and <u>endurance</u>.
   a. tolerance for hardship
   b. vitality
   c. dependability

5. Wolves are intelligent, loving, and <u>loyal</u>.
   a. courageous
   b. faithful
   c. obedient

6. Wolves have <u>complex</u> rules that govern their behavior.
   a. complicated
   b. simple
   c. strange

7. Wolves are famous for their <u>howl</u>.
   a. short, sharp sound
   b. long, loud cry
   c. low, continuous sound

8. Wolves <u>pursue</u> herds of deer.
   a. watch
   b. discover
   c. chase

9. There is much <u>controversy</u> about putting wolves back into the wild.
   a. talk
   b. rumor
   c. argument

10. Many people want to let the wolf <u>roam</u> freely in the wild.
    a. wander about
    b. struggle along
    c. run quickly

USE

Work with a partner to answer the questions. Use complete sentences.

1. What is one thing that a *loyal* friend does?
2. What is an animal other than the wolf that has a *complex* family unit?
3. What is one way to *honor* someone who has done something important?
4. What are two animals that *pursue* their prey?
5. What is the opposite of having *agility*?
6. What are some *rites* that are performed at special occasions in your family?
7. What is a subject of *controversy* in your country or in the world today?
8. What kinds of animals *roam* freely in your country?

COMPREHENSION

 SKIMMING FOR MAIN IDEAS

Quickly read to find the main idea of each paragraph, and then circle the letter of the best answer.

1. Paragraph 2 is mainly about
    a. what the Native Americans believed in.
    b. why the Cheyenne performed the animal dance.
    c. when the Native Americans performed ceremonies.

2. The main topic of paragraph 4 is
    a. the characteristics and habits of the wolf.
    b. how the wolf survives as a social animal.
    c. the relationship between male and female wolves.

3. The main topic of paragraph 6 is
    a. how wolves depend on each other.
    b. the hunting activity of a wolf pack.
    c. what wolves like to eat.

4. The last paragraph is mainly about
    a. why people killed the wolf.
    b. the life of the wolf in Yellowstone National Park.
    c. the argument over putting wolves back into the wild.

SCANNING FOR DETAILS

Reread the passage quickly to find key words and phrases from the questions. Each sentence has an incorrect fact. Cross out the incorrect fact, and write the correct answer above it.

1. Wolves that are found in the far north are often dark red.

2. The Native Americans believed that natural things like mountains and animals had voices in them.

3. The Native Americans admired and depended upon animals, and often gave their friends animal names.

4. Wolves most often hunt alone.

5. The leaders of a wolf pack are the three-year-old wolves.

6. Wolves howl together to share their anger.

7. The most important activity in the pack is raising the young.

8. The pack consists of several females and their young.

9. Wolves are needed to use up the food supply.

10. Wolves usually attack large, healthy deer.

 ## ORDERING EVENTS

Number the sentences to show the correct order. Do this without looking at the passage. Then reread the passage to check your answers.

_____ Wolves are put back into the wild in Yellowstone National Park.

_____ Wolves were hunted and destroyed in great numbers.

_____ Gray wolves live in all parts of North America.

_____ Ranchers and hunters argue against having wolves roam freely in the wild.

_____ The Native Americans respected animals and depended upon them for survival.

_____ European settlers came to America.

★ MAKING INFERENCES AND CONCLUDING

Information is not always stated directly in a passage. Sometimes we make guesses—inferences or conclusions—from the information that is in the reading. The answers to these questions are not directly stated in the passage. Circle the letter of the best answer.

1. From the passage, we can conclude that
   a. wolves are dangerous and frightening animals that should be kept in cages.
   b. wolves are not useful in modern society.
   c. wolves have characteristics that can be admired and respected by humans.

2. We can infer from the passage that
   a. Native Americans were close to nature and knew the characteristics and habits of animals.
   b. Native Americans hunted wolves and were fearful of them.
   c. the settlers killed wolves in large numbers because wolves were killing all the healthy deer they depended on for food.

3. The writer seems to say that
   a. wolves will soon be living in the wild in the large numbers they once were.
   b. it is not likely that wolves will be put back into the wild throughout the United States in the near future.
   c. wolves will probably be extinct in a few years.

DISCUSSION

Discuss the answers to the questions with your classmates.

1. Do you think the wolf should be reintroduced into the wild? Why?
2. People are often described in animal terms, such as "brave as a lion" or "gentle as a lamb." Discuss some of the characteristics of animals and how they are reflected in people.
3. Do you think people should keep wild animals as pets? Why?
4. How have humans upset the balance of nature?

WRITING

Write one or more paragraphs about your favorite animal. Be sure to give specific reasons for your choice.

RESEARCH AND PRESENTATION

Look up the animals in the list below. Find out in what regions of the United States each animal is found, its habitat, and two characteristics of the animal.

1. alligator
2. bald eagle
3. bighorn sheep
4. caribou
5. manatee

6. moose
7. otter
8. rattlesnake
9. roadrunner
10. walrus

Now work with a partner or small group. Prepare a short presentation about one of the animals. Provide facts and characteristics. Talk about whether or not the animal is an endangered species and what is being done to save it. Provide photos, and be prepared to answer questions.

DID YOU KNOW . . . ?
Wolves can run up to 35 miles per hour and jump over something as high as 16 feet!

UNIT 5

Death Valley

Answer the questions.

1. Where are some of the hottest and coldest places in the world?
2. How do you think Death Valley got its name?
3. Would you like to visit a place that is either extremely hot or extremely cold? Why?

Death Valley

1   Death Valley doesn't sound like a very inviting place. It is one of the hottest places in the world. The highest temperature ever recorded there was 134 degrees Fahrenheit. That is the highest ever recorded in the Western Hemisphere, and that was in the shade! Death Valley in California covers nearly 3,000 square miles. Approximately 555 square miles are below the surface of the sea. One point is 282 feet below sea level—the lowest point in the Western Hemisphere. In Death Valley, **pioneers** and explorers faced death from thirst and the **searing** heat. Yet, despite its name and bad reputation, Death Valley is not just an empty wilderness of sand and rock. It is a place of spectacular scenic beauty and home to plants, animals, and even humans.

2   In 1849, a small group of pioneers struggled for three months to get across the rough land. They suffered great hardships as they and their wagons traveled slowly across the **salt flats** in the baking sun. They ran out of food and had to eat their animals and leave their possessions behind. They ran out of water and became so thirsty they could not swallow the meat. They found a lake and fell on their knees, only to discover it was heavily salted. Finally, weak and reduced to almost skeletons, they came upon a spring of fresh water and their lives were saved. When they finally reached the mountains on the other side, they slowly climbed up the rocky slopes. One of them looked back and said, "Good-bye, Death Valley." That has been its name ever since.

3   Death Valley is the driest place in North America. Yet far from being dead, it is alive with plants and animals. They have adapted to this **harsh** region. In the salt flats on the valley floor, there are no plants to be seen, but near the edge, there are grasses. Farther away, there are some small bushes and cactus. On higher ground there are **shrubs** and shrub-like trees. Finally, high on the mountainside, there are pine trees.

4   What is not visible are the seeds **lodged** in the soil, waiting for rain. When it does come, a brilliant display of flowers carpets the once barren flatlands. Even the cactus blossoms. It is the most common of all desert plants. As the water dries up and the hot summer nears, the flowers die, but first they produce seeds that will wait for the rains of another year.

5   At noon on a summer day, Death Valley looks truly **devoid of** wildlife. But in reality, there are fifty-five species of mammals, thirty-two kinds of birds, thirty-six kinds of reptiles, and three kinds of **amphibians**. During the day many seek shelter under rocks and in **burrows**. As night approaches, however, the land cools. The desert becomes a center of animal activity. Owls hunt for mice. Bats gather insects as they fly. The little kit fox is out looking for food, accompanied by snakes, hawks, coyotes, and bobcats. Many of these animals, like the desert plants, have adapted to

the dry desert. They use water very efficiently. They can often survive on water supplies that would leave similar animals elsewhere dying of thirst.

6 Humans have also learned how to survive in this land. Little is known about the first people, the Lake Mohave people, except that they hunted there as long as 9,000 years ago. From 5,000 to 2,000 years ago, the Mesquite Flat people inhabited the region. Then the Saratoga people came. Finally, about 1,000 years ago, the earliest of the Shoshone natives moved in. To this day, a few Shoshone families live the winter months in the desert.

7 The natives knew where every hidden spring was. They also knew the habits of the desert animals, which they hunted. The natives, and later even the prospectors, ate every imaginable desert animal. They ate everything from the bighorn sheep to snakes, rats, and lizards. They were often on the edge of starvation. In autumn they gathered nuts from the pine trees. Other foods they ate included roots, cactus plants, leaves, and sometimes insects.

8 The early prospectors didn't know the desert as well as the natives. Many died looking for gold and silver in Death Valley, but others did find the **precious** metals. Then a "boomtown" was born. First it consisted of miners living in tents, and then permanent buildings were built. But when the mine failed, the town that built up around it did, too. Today the remains of these "ghost towns" are scattered about Death Valley. They have names like Skidoo, Panamint City, Chloride City, and Greenwater.

9 Going to Death Valley once meant danger, hardship, and even death. Today, visitors can drive there in air-conditioned comfort. They can stay in hotels. They don't have to worry about dying of hunger or thirst. They can look upon the hills, canyons, and cactus with appreciation rather than fear. They can admire the beauty of this strange land, and most of all they can leave with happy memories.

VOCABULARY

 MEANING

Complete each definition with one of the following. Guess your answers, and then check them with a dictionary.

pioneers	salt flats	shrubs	devoid of	burrows
searing	harsh	lodged	amphibians	precious

1. Animals that can live both on land and in water are _____.

2. _____ are holes in the ground made by animals and in which the animals live.

3. Intense heat that almost burns is _____.

4. _____ are flat areas covered with salt as a result of water that had been there some time ago and then evaporated.

5. _____ means severe and rough.

6. To be _____ something means to be empty of.

7. _____ are low bushes.

8. _____ are the first settlers in a new or unknown land.

9. Rare and valuable metals such as gold and silver are _____ metals.

10. To be planted firmly or embedded is to be _____.

 USE

Work with a partner to answer the questions. Use complete sentences.

1. What animal is an *amphibian*?
2. Other than a desert, what place looks like it is *devoid of* life?
3. What were some of the hardships faced by people who were *pioneers*?
4. What makes *salt flats*?
5. What are two *precious* gems?
6. Other than Death Valley, what place has *searing* heat?
7. What are two animals that live in *burrows*?
8. What is a place that has *harsh* winters?

COMPREHENSION

 SKIMMING FOR MAIN IDEAS

Quickly read to find the main idea of each paragraph, and then circle the letter of the best answer.

1. The main topic of paragraph 2 is
   a. the hardships a small group of pioneers suffered in Death Valley.
   b. that people have always avoided Death Valley.
   c. that some places in Death Valley are covered with salt.

2. Paragraph 5 is mainly about the fact that
   a. Death Valley is a place full of wildlife.
   b. many kinds of reptiles live in Death Valley.
   c. the animals that live in Death Valley live on desert plants.

3. The main topic of paragraph 6 is
   a. the Lake Mohave people were the earliest and only people who lived in Death Valley.
   b. many peoples have learned to survive in Death Valley.
   c. many native tribes live in Death Valley today.

4. The last paragraph is mainly about
   a. the dangers of going to Death Valley today.
   b. how nature has changed in Death Valley today.
   c. what Death Valley is like for visitors today.

 SCANNING FOR DETAILS

Reread the passage quickly to find key words and phrases from the questions. Then circle the letter of the correct answer.

1. For the early pioneers, crossing Death Valley took as long as
   a. one year.
   b. six months.
   c. three months.

2. Rain in Death Valley causes
   a. flowers to bloom.
   b. minerals to form.
   c. animals to come out and hunt.

3. When prospectors found gold, it often caused
   a. hardship for them.
   b. the soil to be eroded.
   c. a town to be created.

4. Death Valley got its name from
   a. the natives who settled there.
   b. a group of settlers who almost died there.
   c. prospectors who went there.

5. Death Valley is home to plants and animals that have
   a. adapted to the environment.
   b. been brought there by humans.
   c. not been able to survive anyplace else.

6. Settlers could not drink from a lake in Death Valley because
   a. it was salty.
   b. it was empty.
   c. they couldn't reach it.

7. The first people to live in Death Valley were the
   a. Mesquite Flat people.
   b. Lake Mohave people.
   c. Shoshone natives.

8. Of all places in North America, Death Valley is the
   a. highest.
   b. driest.
   c. least populated.

9. The natives could survive in Death Valley because
   a. they didn't stay there all year.
   b. they brought food with them from the mountains.
   c. they knew the location of hidden water.

10. During the day most of the animals in Death Valley
    a. hunt.
    b. find shelter.
    c. eat desert plants.

ORDERING EVENTS

Number the sentences to show the correct order. Do this without looking at the passage. Then reread the passage to check your answers.

_____ A group of pioneers took three months to cross Death Valley.

_____ "Boomtowns" were created.

_____ The Mesquite Flat people lived in Death Valley.

_____ The Saratoga people inhabited Death Valley.

_____ Some mines failed.

_____ The prospectors came looking for gold.

_____ "Ghost towns" were left scattered throughout the desert.

_____ The Lake Mohave people hunted in the region.

MAKING INFERENCES AND CONCLUDING

Information is not always stated directly in a passage. Sometimes we make guesses—inferences or conclusions—from the information that is in the reading. The answers to these questions are not directly stated in the passage. Circle the letter of the best answer.

1. From the passage, we can conclude that
   a. living things have an ability to adapt to the worst environments.
   b. the plants and animals of Death Valley will soon disappear.
   c. mammals make up the smallest part of Death Valley's wildlife population.

2. We can infer from the passage that
   a. people no longer live in Death Valley.
   b. the native peoples didn't settle for very long in Death Valley.
   c. although some prospectors died, others were resourceful enough to live in Death Valley.

3. The writer seems to say that
   a. it was impossible for even the native people to live in Death Valley.
   b. there are no reasons for anyone to go to Death Valley today.
   c. without gold, the pioneers found little reason to live in Death Valley.

DISCUSSION

Discuss the answers to the questions with your classmates.

1. Why do you think people choose to live in places that have harsh conditions?
2. What type of climate does your country have? How have the people there adapted to the climate?
3. If you had to survive on your own in Death Valley, how would you do it?
4. Many scientists say that the world's climate is getting warmer. What do you think the effect of this kind of climate change will be?

WRITING

Write one or more paragraphs that describe what you think would be the ideal place to live. Be sure to give details about the climate and landscape and specific reasons why you would like to live there.

RESEARCH AND PRESENTATION

Find out what the climate is like in each of the following areas of the United States. Name at least two plants and two animals that can be found in each place.

1. The Badlands, South Dakota
2. Bryce Canyon National Park, Utah
3. Cape Cod, Massachusetts
4. The Everglades, Florida
5. Painted Desert, Arizona
6. The Rocky Mountains, Colorado

Now work with a partner or small group. Give a short talk about one of the places you have researched. Provide photos and facts. Be prepared to answer questions.

DID YOU KNOW . . . ?

In Death Valley, the kangaroo rat can live its entire life without drinking a drop of liquid.

38   UNIT 5

Maples and Pecans

PREREADING

Answer the questions.

1. What is your favorite tree?
2. Look at the picture. Why do you think there are containers attached to the tree on the left?
3. What kind of nut trees do you have in your country?

Maples and Pecans

1   Today's national forests are interesting places to camp, hike, and take pictures. But for the Native Americans and early settlers, forests provided their major food sources. In the woods, they hunted animals, fished in lakes and streams, and gathered nuts and berries. They even found a source of sugar. Two trees of great importance to both the natives and settlers were the maple in the northeast and the pecan in the central south.

2   The sugar maple is a tall tree, reaching a height of 75 to 100 feet. It is found in the eastern half of North America, but it is most **abundant** in the forests of New England and southeastern Canada. Its hard wood is often used for furniture and flooring. Its leaves turn red, gold, and orange in the autumn.

3   During the summer, the leaves absorb energy from the sun. This energy is used to manufacture sugar, or glucose. From glucose, the tree creates starch, which it stores in its roots and **trunk**. During the winter, the starch is changed into another sugar, sucrose. It mixes with water to create sap, which flows through the tree in early spring to nourish it as it begins its new growth. The sugar maple has many gallons of sap flowing through it at the end of winter when the days are warm but the nights are still cold.

4   No one knows how the Native Americans discovered the sweet, watery maple sap. But they had many uses for it and stored it in containers they called *mokuks*. When the sap began to flow, or "run," they cut a hole in the bark. Then they put in a wood **chip** to guide the sap into the *mokuk*. This is called "tapping." Native families camped in the maple **grove** until the sap stopped running in the early spring. It was one of their most important foods. A supply of maple sugar saved them from starvation when hunters returned empty-handed. They used it on everything, including meat and fish. They mixed it with corn and wheat to make cakes and a thick soup. They boiled it to make a syrup. Most often they boiled it until it was almost dry, so it could be easily stored.

5   The Native Americans gave the settlers their first taste of maple sugar, and that was all they needed. Soon it became an important food for them, just as it was for the natives. For many New England settlers, it was their only source of sugar. When the words "Sap's running!" were heard, the men quickly gathered their equipment and brought it to the groves. They made holes in the trees and put in wooden **spouts** to guide the sap into their wooden containers. As the containers filled, they carried them to the campsite where they boiled the sap. It was **tedious** work, but an exciting time, too. There was a feeling of spring in the air, and everywhere there was the **aroma** of sweet maple syrup.

6   Maple sugar was a common, everyday sweetener in country kitchens. Today, maple syrup and maple sugar are luxury products. It takes 25 to 30 gallons of sap to produce 1 gallon of syrup. Most candy, ice cream, and pancake syrups have artificial maple flavoring. Maple syrup has become a rare treat, except for those lucky enough to live in a maple grove, of course.

7   While northerners have their maples, southerners have their pecan trees. Pecans are important for their nuts. The central southern area of the United States is the only area of the world where the pecan tree grows wild. Native pecan trees grow in greatest numbers in Texas, Oklahoma, Arkansas, Louisiana, and Mississippi. **Cultivated** pecan trees also produce crops in Georgia, Alabama, New Mexico, North and South Carolina, and Florida.

8   The pecan tree has an average height of 75 feet, although some wild trees have grown as tall as 160 feet. The pecan gets its name from the Native American word *pacanes*, a word the natives used for all nuts with hard shells. The pecan was an important food source for both the natives and settlers. The pecan nuts grow in **clusters** and have reddish-brown shells. The meat of the nut is rich and **nourishing**. It was the custom for natives and settlers to go nutting every autumn. People gathered wild nuts and stored them for winter use.

9   Although there are still some wild nut trees, most of our nuts are grown in groves. Nut trees grow slowly. A few nuts develop on most cultivated trees by age three or four. The pounds of nuts harvested increase with the age of the tree. A fifteen- to twenty-year-old tree produces 75 to 100 pounds. Pecan trees continue producing nuts when they are over 100 years old. One pecan tree in Texas has set a record for producing 1,000 pounds of pecans in one season. That would make quite a pecan pie!

VOCABULARY

MEANING

Complete each definition with one of the following. Guess your answers, and then check them with a dictionary.

abundant	chip	spouts	aroma	clusters
trunk	grove	tedious	cultivated	nourishing

1. A small piece of wood broken off from something is a _____.

2. If something is plentiful, it is _____.

3. The main thick stem of a tree is its _____.

4. The _____ is the characteristic, pleasant smell of something.

5. Work that is _____ is tiring because it is long and boring.

6. When a number of things of the same kind grow in groups, they grow in _____.

7. The place in which a group of fruit or nut trees grows is a _____.

8. If something is _____, it gives food value to your body and is nutritious.

9. Trees that are _____ are grown as crops from seeds.

10. _____ are openings from which liquid comes out, as a small tube or pipe.

 USE

Work with a partner to answer the questions. Use complete sentences.

1. What fruit or flower grows in *clusters*?

2. What are some popular *cultivated* trees?

3. What is a *nourishing* food that you eat every day?

4. Which plant or food do you like the *aroma* of?

5. What kind of work can be *tedious*?

6. What food crop is *abundant* in your country?

7. What is an object that has a *spout*?

8. What are some things that can have a *chip*?

COMPREHENSION

 SKIMMING FOR MAIN IDEAS

Quickly read to find the main idea of each paragraph, and then circle the letter of the best answer.

1. Paragraph 2 is mainly about

   a. the forests of New England and southeastern Canada.

   b. the characteristics of the sugar maple.

   c. the height of the sugar maple.

2. The main topic of paragraph 3 is

   a. what happens to the sugar maple in the summer.

   b. how the sugar maple makes its sugary sap.

   c. why the sugar maple has sugar in the winter.

 **42** UNIT 6

3. The main topic of paragraph 5 is
   a. the importance of maple sugar to the settlers.
   b. the difficulty of making maple syrup.
   c. the equipment needed to extract sap from trees.
4. The last paragraph is mainly about
   a. the amount of nuts older pecan trees produce and how they are used in pies.
   b. the characteristics of the growth and production of nut trees.
   c. the advanced age of some pecan trees.

 ## SCANNING FOR DETAILS

Reread the passage quickly to find key words and phrases from the questions. Then write the correct answer on the line.

1. The Native Americans collected the maple sugar sap in containers called _____ .
2. For many New England settlers, the maple sap was their only source of _____ .
3. The sugar maple tree reaches a height of _____ .
4. The pecan tree was an important food source for both the natives and settlers because _____ .
5. The only area of the world where pecan trees grow wild is _____ _____ .
6. The sap flows in the maple at the end of winter when _____ _____ .
7. Making a hole in the maple tree and putting in a piece of wood to guide the flow of the sap is called _____ .
8. In order to make maple syrup, the sap must be _____ .
9. A twenty-year-old pecan tree produces _____ pounds of pecans in a season.
10. Today, real maple syrup is a luxury item because it takes _____ gallons of sap to make 1 gallon of syrup.

ORDERING EVENTS

Number the sentences to show the correct order. Do this without looking at the passage. Then reread the passage to check your answers.

_____ Sap is boiled to make syrup.

_____ A hole is made in the tree and a spout put in.

_____ Maple leaves absorb energy from the sun.

_____ The sap flows through the tree to nourish its new growth.

_____ The tree changes starch to sucrose.

_____ Sap is collected in containers.

MAKING INFERENCES AND CONCLUDING

Information is not always stated directly in a passage. Sometimes we make guesses—inferences or conclusions—from the information that is in the reading. The answers to these questions are not directly stated in the passage. Circle the letter of the best answer.

1. From the passage, we can conclude that
   a. the settlers did not have to depend upon nature for their survival.
   b. the settlers learned how to use the land's natural resources from the Native Americans.
   c. the settlers had a different way of getting sap from the maple tree than the Native Americans.

2. We can infer from the passage that
   a. the yearly gathering of maple sap was a difficult but rewarding task for the New England settlers.
   b. the New England settlers gathered the maple syrup for pleasure and not out of necessity.
   c. the maple sap was not as important to the Native Americans as it was to the settlers.

3. The writer seems to say that
   a. wild pecan trees produce more nuts than cultivated trees.
   b. pecan trees have a long and productive life.
   c. cultivated trees must be cut down every few years to make room for planting younger trees.

DISCUSSION

Discuss the answers to the questions with your classmates.

1. How do you think the Native Americans may have discovered the maple sap?
2. How important do you think trees are to making a city or town beautiful? Why?
3. If you had a backyard, what type of trees would you put in it? Why?
4. Some trees are known for their beauty, others for their usefulness. Name some in each category.

WRITING

What is the most popular plant in your country? Write one or more paragraphs that describe in detail the plant and ways in which it is used.

RESEARCH AND PRESENTATION

Find out what products are produced from the following trees.

1. baobab
2. eucalyptus
3. jute
4. live oak
5. palm
6. pine

Now work with a partner or small group. Create a poster for one of the trees to show the cycle or process in which the tree produces a product, and present it to your class. Be prepared to answer questions.

DID YOU KNOW . . . ?

There are more than 1,000 varieties of pecans. Many varieties are named after Native American tribes such as Cheyenne, Sioux, and Shawnee.

Oprah Winfrey

PREREADING

Answer the questions.

1. Do you like to watch television talk shows? Why?
2. What is your favorite talk show?
3. What subjects are discussed on talk shows?

Oprah Winfrey

1   Oprah Winfrey is one of the most exciting, highest paid, and best-loved celebrities in America. She is the country's top television talk show host. Oprah Winfrey is a fine actress and a successful producer. She is a living example of what talent, hard work, and determination can do.

2   Oprah has come a long way from her poor childhood home in a small Mississippi town. She was an unwanted child whose parents never married. She was brought up on her grandmother's farm. The possibility that she would become rich and famous was poor.

3   Oprah was left with her grandmother so her mother could go to work in Milwaukee, Wisconsin. Her grandmother was strict and life was difficult for Oprah, but it led the way for her future. She was a highly intelligent child. By the age of three, she had learned to read and write and made her first public appearance. She gave a talk in church, which impressed everyone. "That child is gifted," people said.

4   Other children her age **resented** Oprah's intelligence. They called her unkind names and pushed her away. Oprah felt isolated and unwanted. She felt worse because she didn't live with her mother and father. She thought no one loved her, and she became angry, resentful, and rebellious. These feelings brought her a lot of trouble as she was growing up. She often behaved badly, so her grandmother punished her. By the time Oprah was seven, she was too much for her grandmother to discipline, so Oprah went to live with her mother, Vernita, in Milwaukee.

5   Vernita worked very hard at her job as a housekeeper, and it was difficult to work and take care of her bright, troublesome child. They lived in poverty in a small apartment in the city. Oprah was a burden, and she knew it. Oprah took out all her angry feelings on* her mother. She was so difficult, that when Oprah was eight, Vernita sent her to live with her father and stepmother. She moved again a few months later when Vernita married and wanted Oprah with her and her new family.

6   Unfortunately, Oprah felt she didn't belong there. She believed that no one loved her. Her anger and **frustration** grew. She **struck back** by misbehaving and running away from home. She was impossible to discipline. When she was 14, they wanted to send her to a special center for troubled girls. However, there was no room for her, so Vernita sent Oprah back to live with her father. By then Vernon Winfrey was a successful businessman and family man. He took one look at his daughter and knew she needed **guidance**, love, and discipline. He gave her all three. It was a turning point in Oprah's life. Vernon was strict about his daughter's education. He gave her homework in addition to her

take out on: express one's feelings by making someone else suffer

schoolwork. She could watch only one hour of television a day. She became an A student and a popular girl in her class.

7   Oprah watched Barbara Walters, a famous journalist and interviewer, and decided that was the career she wanted. In high school, she got a part-time job reading news on the radio. During her senior year she won a beauty contest and a four-year scholarship to Tennessee State University. When she was in college, she was offered a job as a news broadcaster at a local television station. She was the first female and the first African-American newscaster in Nashville. In her senior year, she was **promoted** to anchor, the most important position on the news team.

8   After graduation, she got a job with a Baltimore news station, but she soon realized that broadcasting news wasn't for her. She had to let her personality shine through. She wanted to show emotion when she told a story, not just report it. The station managers were feeling the same way. They couldn't stop her from **commenting** on the news she read! They removed her from the anchor spot and wondered what to do with her. Finally, they put her on their early morning talk show, *People Are Talking*. No one knew what to expect.

9   The show was a great success. In a short time, the managers and Oprah all knew what she was born to do. She was funny, **witty**, charming, warm, and **compassionate**. She was everything a **talk show host** should be and was so successful that she got a show, *A.M. Chicago*, with a bigger station. Within one month the show's **ratings** were the best in years. Twice she left the show, to act in the movies *The Color Purple* and *Native Son*. In 1985, the name of the show was changed to *The Oprah Winfrey Show*. It was broadcast nationally and soon became the most popular talk show on television. By the age of 35, Oprah Winfrey was one of the most famous celebrities in America.

10   Today, Oprah's achievements go far beyond being the host of the country's number 1 talk show. She is a film, television, and Broadway play producer, radio programmer, and creator and director of two magazines. She gives millions of dollars to charity and creates education programs and schools worldwide through the Oprah Winfrey Foundation. Oprah has received many awards for her achievements and contributions and has been named one of the 100 most influential people in the world.

VOCABULARY

 MEANING

What is the meaning of the underlined words? Circle the letter of the correct answer. Use a dictionary to check your answers.

1. Other children her age <u>resented</u> her intelligence.
   a. were impressed by
   b. felt angry about
   c. made fun of

2. Her anger and <u>frustration</u> grew stronger.
   a. strong determination
   b. intense dislike
   c. annoyed disappointment

3. She <u>struck back</u> by misbehaving.
   a. went on
   b. responded
   c. held on

4. Oprah's father knew she needed <u>guidance</u>.
   a. help and advice
   b. formal education
   c. punishment and control

5. She was <u>promoted</u> to the position of anchor on the news team.
   a. given a temporary position
   b. transferred
   c. advanced in position

6. They couldn't stop Oprah from <u>commenting</u> on the news.
   a. giving her own opinion
   b. changing the facts
   c. making jokes

7. Oprah was funny, <u>witty</u>, and charming on the show.
   a. tender and loving
   b. clever and humorous
   c. curious about things

8. She was also warm and <u>compassionate</u>.
   a. sympathetic to others
   b. polite to people
   c. amusing

9. Oprah was a great <u>talk show host</u>.
   a. person who gives lectures around the world
   b. person who performs on a television show
   c. person who introduces and interviews people on TV or radio

10. The show had the best <u>ratings</u>.
    a. selection of celebrities
    b. rank given according to popularity
    c. variety of subjects to discuss

USE

Work with a partner to answer the questions. Use complete sentences.

1. What is a profession in which people provide *guidance* for others?
2. What is a characteristic of a *witty* person?
3. Other than Oprah, who is a famous *talk show host* of the past or present?
4. What is one way to get *promoted* in a job?
5. If a person *resented* someone, how might that person behave?
6. What television show currently has high *ratings* in your country?
7. What is a way in which people can be *compassionate* to others?
8. What is something that causes you to have feelings of *frustration*?

COMPREHENSION

 SKIMMING FOR MAIN IDEAS

Quickly read to find the main idea of each paragraph, and then circle the letter of the best answer.

1. Paragraph 3 is mainly about
   a. Oprah's life with her mother.
   b. Oprah's childhood with her grandmother.
   c. Oprah's school years.
2. The main topic of paragraph 5 is that
   a. Oprah was a burden to her mother.
   b. Oprah wanted to live with her father.
   c. Oprah's parents worked hard.
3. Paragraph 7 is mainly about how
   a. Oprah won a beauty contest.
   b. Oprah admired a famous journalist.
   c. Oprah started her career in broadcasting.
4. The main topic of paragraph 9 is that
   a. Oprah became a great success and celebrity.
   b. Oprah starred in two movies.
   c. *A.M. Chicago* got the best ratings after Oprah joined the show.

SCANNING FOR DETAILS

Reread the passage quickly to find key words and phrases from the questions. Then write the correct answer on the line.

1. Oprah's mother left Oprah with her grandmother, so she could go to work in _____ .

2. By the age of three, Oprah had learned _____ .

3. At the age of _____ , Oprah left her grandmother's house and went to live with her mother.

4. Oprah misbehaved so much that when she was fourteen, her parents tried to send her to _____ .

5. Today, Oprah is one of the country's most popular

   _____ .

6. Oprah's life began to change for the better when she went to live with

   _____ .

7. Oprah had roles in two movies: _____ and _____ .

8. In her senior year in high school, Oprah won a scholarship to

   _____ .

9. Before Oprah was given a morning talk show, she had a job as a

   _____ .

10. Oprah's morning talk show was a great success because she was

    funny, _____ , _____ , _____ , and compassionate.

 ORDERING EVENTS

Number the sentences to show the correct order. Do this without looking at the passage. Then reread the passage to check your answers.

_____ Station managers at a Baltimore news station put Oprah on an early morning talk show.

_____ Oprah misbehaved and ran away from home.

_____ Oprah lived on her grandmother's farm in Mississippi.

_____ Oprah's father gave her the guidance and discipline she needed.

_____ Oprah got a part-time job reading news on the radio.

_____ Oprah went to live with her mother in Milwaukee.

_____ Oprah became the first female and the first African-American newscaster in Nashville.

⭐ MAKING INFERENCES AND CONCLUDING

Information is not always stated directly in a passage. Sometimes we make guesses—inferences or conclusions—from the information that is in the reading. The answers to these questions are not directly stated in the passage. Circle the letter of the best answer.

1. From the passage, we can conclude that
   a. Oprah's childhood was easy compared with her adult life.
   b. Oprah's father was an important influence in her life.
   c. Oprah's poor background kept her from achieving her potential.

2. We can infer from the passage that
   a. Oprah's personality made her a better newscaster than a talk show host.
   b. the traits that made Oprah successful appeared at a young age.
   c. Oprah was unable to overcome her problem childhood after she grew up.

3. The writer seems to say that
   a. if Oprah had been a better newscaster, she might have been more successful.
   b. Oprah's personality and intelligence were the two main factors that brought her success.
   c. Oprah's bad behavior as a child was a result of being spoiled by her mother and grandmother.

DISCUSSION

Discuss the answers to the questions with your classmates.

1. The subjects discussed on many talk shows are very personal. Do you think these subjects should be discussed on television? Why?
2. Why do you think talk shows are so popular?
3. If you were a talk show host, who would you like to interview? Why?
4. What factors do you think are important for a person to become rich and famous?

WRITING

Write one or more paragraphs that give at least two reasons for or against having talk shows on television. Be sure to give details that support your reasons.

RESEARCH AND PRESENTATION

Find out what the following African-Americans are famous for.

1. Ray Charles
2. Bill Cosby
3. Whoopie Goldberg
4. Barbara Jordan
5. Rosa Parks
6. Wilma Rudolph

Now work with a partner or small group. Choose a famous African-American and create a biographical presentation with photos about that person. Be prepared to answer questions.

DID YOU KNOW . . . ?

The Oprah Winfrey Show is the longest-running daytime television talk show in the United States.

T-Shirts and Tuxedos

PREREADING

Answer the questions.

1. Do you like to wear T-shirts? Why?
2. What do you wear with T-shirts?
3. When do people wear tuxedos?

T-Shirts and Tuxedos

1   Styles are constantly changing. Fashions come and go, but few have had the popularity or permanence of the T-shirt and tuxedo. Both of these well-known American garments share a history of French influence and American **daring**.

2   The story of the tuxedo goes back to the summer of 1886, in Tuxedo Park, New York. A Frenchman named Pierre Lorillard was living in the small town. He was **heir to** the Lorillard tobacco fortune and an important New York blueblood, a person of high distinction. As always, Pierre had been invited to the Autumn Ball. However, he was tired of wearing the accepted **formal attire** of a coat with **tails**. He wanted something more **informal**, so he asked a tailor to make him several jackets in black without tails. They were modeled after the red riding jackets worn by the British for fox hunting.

3   On the night of the ball, Lorillard was too **timid** to wear one of his tailless dinner jackets, but his son and his young friends were **bolder**. They all put on the jackets and went to the ball. Needless to say, everybody was talking. Their clothing shocked some people. Others, however, were quite interested. They saw how much easier it was to spend the evening in a coat without tails.

4   No doubt, if the tailless coat had been worn by anyone other than a Lorillard, it would never have appeared again. However, because Lorillard had so much influence, tailors started copying the informal jackets. After a while, they became standard evening attire. The tuxedo got its name, of course, from the town in which it was born. The name *Tuxedo* came from the Native Americans. The Algonquians, who had inhabited the area, called it *P'tauk-Seet*, meaning "wolf." The colonists changed it to "Tucksito." By 1800, when Pierre Lorillard's grandfather arrived in the area, the name had already been changed to Tuxedo. In spite of the original meaning of the word, however, good manners are always expected while wearing a tuxedo.

5   T-shirts made their entrance much later than tuxedos, but they, too, took a bit of courage to wear. Once again, the French had a role in the story. It seems the French kept their soldiers cool during World War I by giving them cotton knit undershirts. Meanwhile, the Americans were hot and scratchy in their wool underwear. By World War II, the Navy and Army had learned a lesson from the French. The cotton shirt in a T shape became part of the uniform for all soldiers and sailors. After the war, T-shirts came home with the soldiers. By then, all the men were wearing them, but they remained out of sight, as underwear should in polite society.

6   But Hollywood and rebellious young men know no rules. In 1951, actor Marlon Brando wore a T-shirt in the movie *A Streetcar Named Desire.*

Everyone talked about it, and the T-shirt became a sort of **trademark** for him. Then in the mid-1950s, the young James Dean performed in *Rebel Without a Cause*. He wore a T-shirt, too. Then Elvis Presley hit the screen in his T-shirt. It was too much for young people to ignore. Every boy in town wanted to look like James Dean and Elvis Presley. White T-shirts and **baggy** pants became the "cool," or stylish, thing to wear.

7   The 1960s and another generation of rebellious youth arrived. T-shirts and blue jeans worn by both males and females were their special fashion style. They dyed T-shirts different colors and put pictures and words on them. T-shirts would never be the same again.

8   Today, the T-shirt has made its way to every corner of the world. Infants, teenagers, and senior citizens wear them. They tell others what we like, where we've been, the things we've done, and races we've won. They can be old and worn, or new and fancy. They can be made of cotton or of silk. They're worn with skirts, pants, and shorts. Something that would have surprised even Lorillard is that T-shirts are worn with tuxedos!

VOCABULARY

 MEANING

What is the meaning of the underlined words? Circle the letter of the correct answer. Use a dictionary to check your answers.

1. These garments share a history of French influence and American <u>daring</u>.
   a. spirit
   b. bravery
   c. style

2. Pierre Lorillard was <u>heir to</u> a tobacco fortune.
   a. the one who inherits property
   b. the manager of
   c. the father of

3. Pierre Lorillard was tired of wearing <u>formal</u> clothes
   a. as accepted by rules or customs
   b. old-fashioned
   c. of the latest fashion

4. The accepted <u>attire</u> for the ball was a coat with tails.
   a. costume
   b. clothing
   c. uniform

5. Men wore a coat with <u>tails</u> to the Autumn Ball.
   a. a coat with a long collar
   b. a coat with two long lower-back parts
   c. a coat with a lot of buttons

6. Pierre Lorillard wanted to wear something <u>informal</u>.
   a. different
   b. casual
   c. unique

7. Lorillard was too <u>timid</u> to wear his tailless dinner jacket.
   a. lacking in courage
   b. excited
   c. proud

8. His son and his friends were <u>bolder</u>.
   a. more dependable
   b. more impolite
   c. more courageous

9. The T-shirt became a kind of <u>trademark</u> for Marlon Brando.
   a. symbol
   b. tradition
   c. legend

10. Young people wanted to wear white T-shirts and <u>baggy</u> pants.
    a. loose
    b. tight
    c. short

 USE

Work with a partner to answer the questions. Use complete sentences.

1. What kind of clothes do *bold* people wear?
2. What is *formal* clothing for women?
3. What clothing is or was a *trademark* for a famous person?
4. What is a formal event to which men once wore *tails*?
5. What are three *informal* pieces of clothing that people wear today?
6. What person is or was an *heir to* a great fortune?
7. What are two characteristics of a *daring* person?
8. Why do many people like to wear *baggy* clothing?

COMPREHENSION

 SKIMMING FOR MAIN IDEAS

Quickly read to find the main idea of each paragraph, and then circle the letter of the best answer.

1. Paragraph 2 is mainly about
   a. how a rich man named Pierre Lorillard lived in a small town.
   b. the story of how the tuxedo began.
   c. what people wore to the Autumn Ball in Tuxedo Park.

2. The main topic in paragraph 5 is
   a. what soldiers wore during World War I.
   b. how the T-shirt got its name.
   c. when T-shirts started to be worn.

3. The main topic in paragraph 6 is
   a. how Hollywood made the T-shirt popular.
   b. what Marlon Brando wore in a movie.
   c. why boys wanted to look like Elvis Presley and James Dean.
4. The last paragraph is mainly about
   a. how T-shirts are worn by people of all ages.
   b. the popularity of the T-shirt today.
   c. the different kinds of T-shirts people wear.

 SCANNING FOR DETAILS

Reread the passage quickly to find key words and phrases from the questions. Circle *T* if the sentence is true. Circle *F* if the sentence is false.

1. The word *tuxedo* comes from a Native American word meaning "wolf."	T	F
2. Pierre Lorillard asked his tailors to make him a tailless jacket to wear when he went hunting.	T	F
3. Although Pierre Lorillard thought up the idea of the tailless jacket, he wasn't the first person to wear it.	T	F
4. The first person to wear a T-shirt on the movie screen was James Dean.	T	F
5. Pierre Lorillard's family were bankers.	T	F
6. When Lorillard's son and his friends wore the tailless jackets, everyone loved them.	T	F
7. The T-shirt originated with the French military.	T	F
8. In the 1960s, colored T-shirts with words printed on them came into style.	T	F
9. In the 1950s, T-shirts and baggy pants were "cool."	T	F
10. Pierre Lorillard's grandfather gave Tuxedo Park its name.	T	F

⭐ ORDERING EVENTS

Number the sentences to show the correct order. Do this without looking at the passage. Then reread the passage to check your answers.

____ Elvis Presley wore a T-shirt in his movies.

____ Lorillard asked his tailors to make several dinner jackets without tails.

____ T-shirts became part of the American military uniform.

____ Pierre Lorillard's grandfather arrived in America.

____ T-shirts and blue jeans became the fashion.

____ Tailors began to make copies of Lorillard's tailless jacket.

____ Lorillard's son wore the tailless jacket to the Autumn Ball.

____ French soldiers wore cotton undershirts.

⭐ MAKING INFERENCES AND CONCLUDING

Information is not always stated directly in a passage. Sometimes we make guesses—inferences or conclusions—from the information that is in the reading. The answers to these questions are not directly stated in the passage. Circle the letter of the best answer.

1. From the passage, we can conclude that
   a. fashions are often started by the military.
   b. most fashions start with large groups of people who wear certain clothing for practical reasons.
   c. fashions often become popular when they are worn by someone people admire.

2. We can infer from the passage that
   a. the tuxedo would have been popular no matter who created it.
   b. T-shirts and tuxedos were both ignored when they were first worn.
   c. the influence of Hollywood made T-shirts outerwear instead of underwear.

3. The writer seems to say that
   a. the clothes we wear say something about ourselves.
   b. fashions are often started by people who want to look like everyone else.
   c. new fashions are usually worn by adults before they become popular with young people.

DISCUSSION

Discuss the answers to the questions with your classmates.

1. What is the fashion this year? Do you like it? Why?
2. If you were a fashion designer, what fashion style would you create for next year?
3. If you could print anything you wanted on your T-shirt, what would you put on it? Why?
4. Do you like to wear designer clothes? Why?

WRITING

Write one or more paragraphs that give reasons for or against wearing the current fashion styles.

RESEARCH AND PRESENTATION

Find out where each of the following items of clothing came from and how they are worn.

1. blue jeans
2. clogs
3. kilt
4. kimono
5. sneakers
6. Stetson

Now work with a partner or small group. Choose one item of clothing and prepare a presentation that gives the history of that item, as well as how and when it is worn. Include photos or the authentic clothing. Be prepared to answer questions.

DID YOU KNOW . . . ?

Ninety-one percent of Americans say they own a "favorite" T-shirt, and 62 percent say they own more than ten T-shirts, which adds up to 1.5 billion T-shirts. If they were lined up, they'd circle the globe thirty-four times!

The Wright Brothers Take Off

PREREADING

Answer the questions.

1. What are some of the ways in which people can fly?
2. Do you like to fly? Why?
3. Would you like to own your own airplane? Why?

The Wright Brothers Take Off

1   From the time of primitive man, humans have wanted to fly. Centuries ago men **strapped** wings on themselves in an attempt to fly. Needless to say, more than one leg was broken trying that. By 1900, humans had finally succeeded in flying through the air. They had done it in balloons and **gliders**. Now they were ready for the next step.

2   Two brothers, Orville and Wilbur Wright, owned a bicycle shop in Dayton, Ohio, and loved mechanical things. They were also fascinated with the idea of flying. They had read about the glider experiments of Otto Lilienthal, a German inventor, and Octave Chanute, a French-born American engineer. They decided to make a glider of their own. They came up with a biplane, or double-wing glider. It had a new **feature** called "wing warping," a way of bending the wings to make the best use of air flowing over them. They made several successful flights with their biplane glider, but the Wright brothers wanted more.

3   They asked the U.S. Weather Bureau where the strongest and steadiest winds blew; strong winds were necessary for glider flying. As Orville and Wilbur and other glider pilots knew, when the winds stopped, the plane went down. In the fall of 1900, the Wright brothers took a new glider to the windy beaches near Kitty Hawk, North Carolina. It had bent wings and a **flap** in front for better up-and-down movement. Once again, their glider was successful. Once again, it wasn't quite good enough.

4   The Wright brothers went back to their home in Dayton. They set up a wind tunnel to test the data that Lilienthal and Chanute had **come up with** in their glider experiments. The wind tests showed the figures were wrong. The Wright brothers had more designing to do.

5   In 1902, Orville and Wilbur were back in Kitty Hawk with a redesigned glider. This one had straighter wings, a movable **rudder**, and better control. They made more than a thousand successful flights on the deserted beaches. However, the Wright brothers weren't happy with having to rely on nature and its unpredictable winds. They wanted more. They wanted powered flight.

6   No engine on the market was light and powerful enough for an airplane, so they built their own. There were no **propellers** around either, so they built them, too. They put one propeller behind the engine and one behind the pilot. Power from the engine was carried to the propellers by a bicycle chain.

7   The brothers went back and forth to Kitty Hawk. With each unsuccessful flight, they corrected the problem and tried again. On December 17, 1903, they were ready for another try. They had named their odd-looking, two-winged **contraption** *Flyer*. It was a cold, windy day. No one, except four men and a boy, was interested enough to watch the

Wright brothers try their funny flying machine. No one believed that humans would ever fly a mechanical plane.

8   The brothers always took turns at piloting their experimental airplanes. That day, Orville climbed into *Flyer* and lay flat on the lower wing. He started the engine and the plane moved forward. Then it lifted off the ground, reaching 40 feet. Orville found the controls so sensitive that when he changed the angle of the controls just a little, the plane rose or fell sharply. Then he altered one of the controls a little too much, and the plane came down. It had flown 120 feet and had been in the air for twelve seconds. History had been made. What humankind had dreamed about for thousands of years had finally become reality.

9   The Wright brothers made three more flights that day. The fourth flight lasted fifty-nine seconds and went a distance of 852 feet. After that flight, everyone gathered around the aircraft. They joyfully discussed what had happened. Suddenly a strong **gust** of wind picked up the plane and turned it over and over while everyone watched in **dismay**. It was badly damaged and could not be flown again that day. The Wright brothers were not sad, however, because they had accomplished their goal.

10   In spite of this great historical achievement, the Wright brothers and their flight went nearly unnoticed. They continued their research and experimentation for almost three more years. Finally, they were granted a U.S. patent on their plane in 1906. In 1907, they went to Europe and flew their aircraft from place to place, to the delight of thousands of Europeans. The success of this tour reached American newspapers. The Wright brothers finally achieved their long-deserved fame and honor. The door was opened to the future, and it took Americans only sixty-six years to go from the beaches of Kitty Hawk to the distant moon.

VOCABULARY

 MEANING

What is the meaning of the underlined words? Circle the letter of the correct answer. Use a dictionary to check your answers.

1. A long time ago, men <u>strapped</u> on wings in order to fly.
   a. sewed with thread
   b. fastened with bands or belts
   c. stuck with glue

2. Men had flown in balloons and <u>gliders</u>.
   a. planes without engines
   b. planes attached to balloons
   c. balloons with metal frames

3. The new plane had a <u>feature</u> called "wing warping."
   a. special comment or report
   b. special gift or favor
   c. special part or quality

4. The glider had bent wings and a <u>flap</u> in front.
   a. handle
   b. movable edge
   c. wooden support

5. The Wright brothers tested what other inventors had <u>come up with</u> in their experiments.
   a. dreamed about
   b. found out
   c. taken up

6. The glider had a movable <u>rudder</u>.
   a. blade at the back that controls the direction
   b. instrument that indicates speed
   c. seat for the pilot

7. There were no <u>propellers</u> for their airplane.
   a. controls for the pilot
   b. blades that are turned at a high speed by the engine
   c. wings that move up and down mechanically

8. The brothers called their <u>contraption</u> *Flyer.*
   a. small motor
   b. well-designed engine
   c. strange-looking machine

9. A <u>gust</u> of wind picked up the plane.
   a. sudden, strong rush of air
   b. soft breeze
   c. air that swirls like a cyclone

10. People watched in <u>dismay</u>.
    a. alarm
    b. suspicion
    c. delight

 USE

Work with a partner to answer the questions. Use complete sentences.

1. What unique experience does flying in *gliders* provide?
2. Other than an airplane, what is something that has a *rudder*?
3. What kind of person would make a *contraption*?
4. What is a *feature* that you like and one you dislike about modern passenger planes?
5. Other than an airplane, what is something that uses *propellers*?
6. How does a person show *dismay*?
7. What happens when a *gust* of wind comes down a street?
8. What is something into which people are *strapped*?

COMPREHENSION

SKIMMING FOR MAIN IDEAS

Quickly read to find the main idea of each paragraph, and then circle the letter of the best answer.

1. Paragraph 5 is mainly about
   a. the Wright brothers going back to Kitty Hawk.
   b. the Wright brothers making more than a thousand flights.
   c. the dissatisfaction of the brothers with their glider.

2. Paragraph 6 is mostly about the fact that
   a. the brothers built their own engine and propellers.
   b. the brothers put the propellers behind the engine and pilot.
   c. the power from the engine went to the propellers.

3. The main topic of paragraph 8 is that
   a. the *Flyer* went 120 feet on its first flight.
   b. the Wright brothers made an historical achievement.
   c. the controls of the *Flyer* were very sensitive.

4. The last paragraph is mainly about the fact that
   a. the Wright brothers were granted a patent.
   b. the Wright brothers finally got their long-deserved fame.
   c. it took Americans sixty-six years to go from Kitty Hawk to the moon.

SCANNING FOR DETAILS

Reread the passage quickly to find key words and phrases from the questions. Each sentence has an incorrect fact. Cross out the incorrect fact, and write the correct answer above it.

1. The Wright brothers discovered that Lilienthal's and Chanute's data were accurate.

2. The first plane the Wright brothers made was a single-wing airship.

3. Orville and Wilbur Wright owned a motorcycle shop in Dayton, Ohio.

4. The Wright brothers tested their planes near Kitty Hawk, South Carolina.

5. The Wright brothers bought their propellers and engine for their plane.

6. "Wing warping" was a way of straightening the airplane's wings.

7. The Wright brothers put a cockpit on their plane for better control.

8. The first successful flight of the *Flyer* lasted ten seconds and went a distance of 200 feet.

9. In 1907 the Wright brothers traveled all over America in their airplane.

10. A crowd saw the *Flyer* make history on December 17, 1903.

 ORDERING EVENTS

Number the sentences to show the correct order. Do this without looking at the passage. Then reread the passage to check your answers.

_____ Orville and Wilbur used a wind tunnel to make tests.

_____ Men strapped wings to their arms in an attempt to fly.

_____ Orville and Wilbur Wright built a glider.

_____ The *Flyer* was damaged.

_____ The Wright brothers made the world's first flight in a motorized plane.

_____ Lilienthal and Chanute experimented with gliders.

_____ The Wright brothers were given a U.S. patent for their plane.

 MAKING INFERENCES AND DRAWING CONCLUSIONS

Information is not always stated directly in a passage. Sometimes we make guesses—inferences or conclusions—from the information that is in the reading. The answers to these questions are not directly stated in the passage. Circle the letter of the best answer.

1. From the passage, we can conclude that
   a. fame and fortune came easily to the Wright brothers.
   b. the first flight of the *Flyer* disappointed the Wright brothers.
   c. the Wright brothers were determined to make their dream come true.

2. We can infer from the passage that
   a. although the *Flyer* made history with its first successful flight, the Wright brothers still had many improvements to make on its design.
   b. before the Wright brothers, no one had made any achievements in flying.
   c. very few people had any interest in the idea of flying until 1902.

3. The writer seems to say that
   a. Europeans were responsible for inventing the motorized plane.
   b. the U.S. Weather Bureau played an important role in the invention of the first glider.
   c. after the Wright brothers flew their motorized plane for the first time, Americans did not appreciate the importance of what they had done.

DISCUSSION

Discuss the answers to the questions with your classmates.

1. Why do you think some people have a fear of flying?
2. How has the invention of jet planes affected our lives?
3. What other inventions in transportation have affected our lives?
4. What do you think passenger planes will be like in the future?

WRITING

Write one or more paragraphs about your favorite form of transportation. Be sure to give reasons to support your point of view.

RESEARCH AND PRESENTATION

Find out what form of air travel the following people invented.

1. Sir George Cayley   2. Henri Giffard   3. Wernher von Braun

Now work with a partner or small group. Give a short presentation about the form of air travel that one person invented. Include photos or drawings in your presentation. Be prepared to answer questions.

DID YOU KNOW . . . ?
Joseph and Etienne Montgolfier designed the first successful flying craft. They put hot air and gas into a balloon and attached a basket to it. The world's first aviators were inside—a duck, rooster, and a sheep!

The Mystery of Roanoke Island

PREREADING

Answer the questions.

1. Do you like mysteries? Why?
2. What mysterious places do you know?
3. What people do you know whose life or death involves mystery?

The Mystery of Roanoke Island

1   Everyone loves a mystery. Books, stories, movies, and television programs involving mysteries are very popular. Fictional mysteries are fun to try to solve before the author finally reveals the secret. However, there are many real-life mysteries that have never been solved. One of them is the mystery of the "Lost Colony" of Roanoke.

2   The story begins in 1585. An English explorer named Sir Walter Raleigh wanted to start settlements in the New World for his glory and that of his queen, Elizabeth I. Raleigh sent 108 men to settle on Roanoke Island, off the coast of Virginia.* However, these men were soldiers and didn't know how to farm. They quickly ran out of food. By 1586 the settlers were sick and starving.

3   One day some English ships **anchored** near the island. The captains of these ships agreed to take the settlers back to England. The settlers brought back with them Indian corn and potatoes, which were unknown in England. Sir Walter Raleigh planted the potatoes on his estate in Ireland. Later they became a chief source of food for the Irish people.

4   Raleigh was still determined to start a colony in Virginia. This time he decided to include farmers and families who could build things and survive in their settlement. In 1587, he sent 150 men, women, and children in three ships across the sea. Many had sold everything they owned in hopes of a better life in the New World. The ships were on their way to Chesapeake Bay, where it was thought a settlement could be more successful than on Roanoke Island. However, the captain of the expedition stopped at Roanoke and refused to take the passengers any farther. They had no choice but to settle on the island.

5   They repaired the old **fort** and began to build cabins, but they soon realized they would need many more supplies than they had brought with them. It was decided that their leader and governor, John White, would go back to England for help and more **provisions**. A week before he sailed, White's daughter gave birth to a baby girl—the first English child to be born in America. Her name was Virginia Dare. Because conditions on the island were difficult, some of the settlers wanted to move to another place. Before Governor White left, he told them that if they left the island, they should **carve** on a tree the name of the place where they were going. If they had troubles, they should put a cross above the name.

6   Upon reaching England, White discovered that England was at war with Spain. Every ship in the country was needed. He and Sir Walter Raleigh tried in every way to send ships to the **stranded** little colony

---

Virginia: In 1585, Virginia was a region much larger than the present state of the same name. Today, Roanoke Island is in the state of North Carolina.

across the sea. But it was not to be. Three years passed before White was able to return to Roanoke Island.

7   In August of 1590, the governor stepped ashore at Roanoke. He walked to the settlement with fear in his heart. Upon reaching it, he found only **deserted ruins**. The cabins had been destroyed, and the ground was overgrown with high grass and weeds. He found rusted pieces of metal and **moldy** books. It was obvious the colony had been **abandoned** for at least a year.

8   White was deeply troubled. But then, at the entrance to the settlement, he saw the word *CROATOAN* carved in a tree. There was no cross above the word. Croatoan was the name of a nearby island inhabited by a friendly native tribe. White was confident the settlers would be found.

9   The ship's captain agreed to sail to Croatoan the next morning, but during the night, there was a terrible storm. The ship lost all but one anchor. The captain was more concerned for his ship than for the colonists, so he sailed away from the storm. The storm, however, followed and blew them far into the Atlantic. The captain refused to go back, so White unhappily was taken back to England.

10   Although several search parties were eventually sent to Roanoke and Croatoan, not one clue to the fate of the settlers was ever found. Governor White would never know what happened to his daughter and grandchild, or all the others who had so bravely made the journey with him.

11   **Ironically**, the fate of Governor White also became a mystery. It is not known where or when he died. There is a record that in 1606 a man named John White died "in parts beyond the sea." It seems very likely that White died still searching for the men and women he had left with a promise of help, but was unable to save.

VOCABULARY

MEANING

What is the meaning of the underlined words? Circle the letter of the correct answer. Use a dictionary to check your answers.

1. Some English ships <u>anchored</u> near Roanoke Island.
   a. were unable to sail because there was no wind
   b. hit upon some rocks and then repaired the ships
   c. stayed in one place

2. The settlers repaired the old <u>fort</u>.
   a. strongly made building used for defense
   b. roughly made school
   c. strongly made bridge

3. John White went back to England for help and <u>provisions</u>.
   a. settlers
   b. soldiers
   c. supplies
4. He told them to <u>carve</u> the name of their destination on a tree.
   a. cut
   b. paint
   c. attach
5. They tried to send ships to the <u>stranded</u> colony across the sea.
   a. created for a special purpose
   b. left in a helpless position
   c. populated by a few people
6. The governor found <u>deserted</u> ruins.
   a. dried up
   b. empty
   c. ancient
7. He found <u>ruins</u>.
   a. household objects
   b. remains of buildings
   c. uncared for fields
8. The books were <u>moldy</u>.
   a. covered with a greenish growth
   b. filled with pictures
   c. dried up
9. The colony had been <u>abandoned</u> for at least a year.
   a. left empty
   b. destroyed
   c. occupied
10. <u>Ironically</u>, the fate of Governor White became a mystery, too.
    a. unexpectedly
    b. unfortunately
    c. interestingly

 USE

Work with a partner to answer the questions. Use complete sentences.
1. What kind of food often gets *moldy*?
2. What are two characteristics of a *fort*?
3. Where are ships often *anchored*?
4. What would you do if you were *stranded* on a deserted island?
5. What happens to *abandoned* places over time?
6. What *provisions* would you take if you were going to a place where there was no civilization?
7. What is a material other than wood on which people like to *carve*?
8. What is a famous place that has *ruins* of a past civilization?

COMPREHENSION

SKIMMING FOR MAIN IDEAS

Quickly read to find the main idea of each paragraph, and then circle the letter of the best answer.

1. The main topic of paragraph 4 is
   a. how Raleigh tried to start a successful colony.
   b. why people sold everything they owned.
   c. why farmers were needed in the colony.

2. The main topic of paragraph 7 is that
   a. the governor became afraid at Roanoke.
   b. the governor found Roanoke deserted.
   c. the settlement was overgrown with grass.

3. Paragraph 10 is mainly about
   a. what the search parties found at Roanoke.
   b. no one knowing what happened to the settlers.
   c. the governor's search for his daughter.

4. The main topic of the last paragraph is
   a. the mystery of what happened to Governor White.
   b. the death of Governor White at sea.
   c. White's search for the men and women at Roanoke.

SCANNING FOR DETAILS

Reread the passage quickly to find key words and phrases from the questions. Circle *T* if the sentence is true. Circle *F* if the sentence is false.

1. Governor White's granddaughter was the first English child born in America.   T   F

2. The first settlers on Roanoke did not have the skills to survive in the wilderness.   T   F

3. Governor White left Roanoke because he wanted to go fight for the British Navy.   T   F

4. Governor White couldn't return to Roanoke because Sir Walter Raleigh had lost interest in the colony.   T   F

5. It was five years before Governor White could return to Roanoke. T F

6. Sir Walter Raleigh was mostly interested in importing plants from the New World. T F

7. Most of the colonists went to Roanoke with the intention of eventually returning to England. T F

8. The colonists left a message saying where they had gone. T F

9. Governor White died a lonely death in England. T F

10. When Governor White finally returned to Roanoke, he found all the buildings still standing, but the colonists were no longer there. T F

 ORDERING EVENTS

Number the sentences to show the correct order. Do this without looking at the passage. Then reread the passage to check your answers.

_____ The settlers needed more supplies for the colony.

_____ Governor White found the remains of the settlement.

_____ Sir Walter Raleigh sent 108 men to settle on Roanoke.

_____ Three ships brought settler families to Roanoke.

_____ Search parties were sent to find the missing colonists.

_____ Indian corn and potatoes were taken to England and Ireland.

_____ Governor White left for England.

 MAKING INFERENCES AND CONCLUDING

Information is not always stated directly in a passage. Sometimes we make guesses—inferences or conclusions—from the information that is in the reading. The answers to these questions are not directly stated in the passage. Circle the letter of the best answer.

1. From the passage, we can conclude that
   a. Roanoke Island was not the best place to try to start a colony.
   b. Roanoke Island was rich in natural resources.
   c. it wasn't necessary for Governor White to leave Roanoke.

2. We can infer from the passage that
   a. Governor White didn't like Sir Walter Raleigh.
   b. Governor White was not planning to return to the colony after he left.
   c. Governor White felt the colony couldn't survive without more supplies.

3. The writer seems to say that
   a. if Governor White had stayed on Roanoke, the colony would have been a success.
   b. storms probably drove the colonists off Roanoke.
   c. when the colonists left Roanoke, they were probably not in danger.

DISCUSSION

Discuss the answers to the questions with your classmates.

1. Do you think Governor White should have left the settlers? Why?
2. What do you think happened to Governor White?
3. There are many mysteries concerning outer space. Do you believe there is life on other planets? Do you think other beings or aliens have visited Earth? Why?
4. Do you believe in spirits? Give reasons.

WRITING

Write one or more paragraphs about what you think happened to the settlers in Roanoke. Give at least one reason for your opinion.

RESEARCH AND PRESENTATION

Choose one of the following mysteries. Find out when, where, and what the mystery is.

1. Atlantis
2. Bermuda Triangle
3. Crop Circles
4. Macchu Picchu
5. The Nazca lines
6. Stonehenge

Now work with a partner or small group. Make a presentation about one mystery to your class. Be prepared to answer questions.

DID YOU KNOW . . . ?

A famous mystery in the United States involves the actor James Dean, who was killed in his Porsche Spyder in 1955. Anyone who came in contact with the car or its parts afterward suffered injuries or death until the vehicle finally mysteriously disappeared.

Getting on Board

PREREADING

Answer the questions.

1. Is skateboarding, windsurfing, or snowboarding popular in your country? In what areas?
2. Do you participate in any of these sports? If not, would you like to? Why?
3. Why do you think these sports are so popular?

Getting on Board

1   On water, streets, and snow, millions of Americans get on their sailboards, skateboards, and snowboards and experience the excitement of speed. Every year, the number of boarders—people who ride boards—goes up. Young and old, **amateur** and professional, more and more people get on boards for a day of fun or extreme competition.

2   Skateboarding is the oldest of the three sports. In the early 1900s, roller-skating was popular. Roller skates had four wheels. Boys liked to **take apart** their skates, attach them to a small board, and put a wooden box on the board. They attached a long stick or piece of wood to hold onto, and created the first homemade scooters. After a while, the boys started removing the box, riding only on the board, and calling it a skateboard.

3   In the 1950s, two surfers, Bill Richards and his son Mark, had the idea that skateboards could be used to "surf" on the sidewalk when they couldn't surf in the water. Other surfers loved the idea, and soon manufacturers were making skateboards and selling them in department stores. Skateboarding spread across the country.

4   Until the early 1970s, skateboards were slow and skateboarders couldn't **do tricks**. But in 1973, a surfer named Frank Nasworthy invented wheels made of urethane, a hard plastic. Skateboarding was never the same! Skateboarders went faster and could do jumps and turns. They learned to fly through the air, twist, turn, and do all kinds of tricks. By the mid-1980s, skateboarding was becoming a serious sport, and it wasn't just for kids. Competitions were organized, and skateboarding spread across the **globe**.

5   Today skateboarding is a professional sport. There are international competitions, money, and fame for the greatest boarders. Everybody loves to watch the wild tricks of the skateboarders in the X Games, a type of small Olympics for extreme sports. But skateboarding has never stopped being a great way for kids to get down the street.

6   Where there are sidewalks there are skateboards, and where there is wind and water, there are sailboards—large surfboards with sails attached. In 1968, two men from southern California got patents for the first sailboard, or "windsurfer." Jim Drake was a sailor, and Hoyle Schweitzer was a surfer. Together they came up with the idea to combine their two sports. They designed a special way to attach the sail to the board, took their invention out on the water, and windsurfing was born. From that point on, windsurfers moved across the water and reached amazing speeds. They started jumping, twisting, turning, and riding huge waves.

7   It didn't take long for windsurfing to become popular in Europe, Australia, and other places. Windsurfers and their equipment got better

and better. In 1983, the professional World Cup tour was started. In 1984, windsurfing became an Olympic sport of the Summer Games. Today the joys and **thrill of** windsurfing are experienced by millions of people around the world.

8   Another board sport that goes back to the 1960s is snowboarding. In Michigan in 1965, a man named Sherman Poppen had a great idea for his children. He **fastened** a pair of children's skis together, put a rope in the front, and watched his daughter happily **slide down** a hill. He called his invention the Snurfer, a **combination of** snow and surf. Soon all the neighborhood children were asking Poppen to make them one. After a while, Poppen sold his idea to a sports equipment manufacturer. By the mid-1970s, almost half a million Snurfers had been sold.

9   In the late 1970s, the Snurfer was improved. Dimitrije Milovich, Tom Sims, Chris Sanders, Mike Olson, and Jack Burton all introduced new designs that eventually developed into today's snowboard. By the mid-1980s, snowboarding was becoming popular around the world. Championship competitions were held in Europe and America. As time passed, the boards got better, and the boarders improved, too. Soon they were speeding down hills and over jumps, **doing flips** in the air and other amazing tricks.

10   As popular as snowboarding was, most ski **resorts** didn't allow snowboarding until the 1990s. Resort owners thought the snowboarders couldn't control their boards and would cause accidents. Most snowboarders were young people, and they had their own culture. They wore baggy pants and jackets, and they listened to loud music. They liked to have fun and do wild tricks, but resort owners were very traditional. They were afraid to let boarders on the mountain. When they did, sometimes there was trouble between the skiers and boarders. The skiers didn't like the snowboarders on the slopes with them. Some boarders were rude, didn't follow the rules, and sometimes caused problems. After a while, though, resort owners realized that snowboarders would bring money to their areas. One after another, they let snowboarders in. Snowboarding grew faster than skiing. Resorts welcomed the new business. They built areas with jumps and special courses for snowboarders. Many skiers learned to snowboard too, and skiers and snowboarders began to understand and respect each other.

11   In 1998, snowboarding joined the Olympic Winter Games in Nagano, Japan. Today, fans can also watch boarders fly through the air at the Winter X Games. They can get on a board themselves and enjoy the thrill of speeding down a mountain. Every year the number of snowboarders grows in countries around the world. It seems that everyone loves this new and exciting sport.

VOCABULARY

MEANING

What is the meaning of the underlined words? Circle the letter of the correct answer. Use a dictionary to check your answers.

1. Both <u>amateur</u> and professional people ride sailboards, skateboards, and snowboards.
   a. a person with a lot of training and education in a particular area
   b. a person who truly enjoys doing a certain activity
   c. a person without much experience or skill in a certain area

2. Boys liked to <u>take apart</u> their skates.
   a. add new pieces to
   b. separate into pieces
   c. put pieces together

3. People couldn't <u>do tricks</u> on the early skateboards.
   a. do something without any difficulty
   b. have fun with something
   c. perform actions that take a special skill

4. Skateboarding spread across the <u>globe</u>.
   a. country
   b. world
   c. universe

5. Millions of people experience the <u>thrill of</u> windsurfing.
   a. fear related to
   b. excitement in connection with
   c. difficulty experienced by

6. Poppen <u>fastened</u> a pair of skis together.
   a. bent strongly
   b. separated slightly
   c. joined firmly

7. Poppen watched his daughter <u>slide down</u> a hill.
   a. move smoothly toward the bottom
   b. move quickly to the top
   c. move along with a lot of shaking

8. The name Snurfer is a <u>combination of</u> snow and surf.
   a. mixture or blend of
   b. part or portion of
   c. division or separation of

9. Boarders were soon <u>doing flips</u> in the air.
   a. bending backward
   b. turning over
   c. jumping

10. Most ski <u>resorts</u> didn't allow snowboarding at first.
   a. places where people go to get special training
   b. places where people go to watch professional sports
   c. places where people go to enjoy themselves

 USE

Work with a partner to answer the questions. Use complete sentences.

1. What are some jobs that require workers to *take apart* things?
2. What are some words that are a *combination of* two words?
3. What are some of your favorite places around the *globe*?
4. What is the main difference between an *amateur* and a professional?
5. What are some animals that can *do tricks*?
6. What are some things that give people the *thrill of* going fast?
7. Why do people like to go to *resorts*?
8. What are some ways in which people *slide down* hills?

COMPREHENSION

 SKIMMING FOR MAIN IDEAS

Quickly read to find the main idea of each paragraph, and then circle the letter of the best answer.

1. Paragraph 2 is mainly about
   a. how popular roller-skating was in the early twentieth century.
   b. how children took apart their skates.
   c. how boys made the first skateboards.

2. The main topic of paragraph 6 is
   a. how Drake and Schweitzer got patents for their first sailboard.
   b. the things people can do on sailboards.
   c. how windsurfing got started.

3. The main topic of paragraph 9 is
   a. the people who helped to design the first snowboard.
   b. the development of snowboarding.
   c. the snowboarding competitions.
4. Paragraph 10 is mainly about
   a. the differences between skiers and snowboarders.
   b. the changes in attitude of resort owners toward snowboarders.
   c. the rising popularity of snowboarding.

 SCANNING FOR DETAILS

Reread the passage quickly to find key words and phrases from the questions. Then write the correct answer on the line.

1. The oldest of the three sports is _____.
2. The wheels for the first skateboards came from _____.
3. Bill Richards and his son got the idea to skateboard on sidewalks when

   _____.

4. After Frank Nasworthy invented _____,

   skateboards were faster.
5. The X Games is _____.
6. Drake and Schweitzer got the idea to combine the two sports of

   _____.

7. In the year _____, windsurfing became an Olympic sport.
8. Poppen created the Snurfer by fastening a pair of skis together and

   putting a _____ in front.
9. Tom Sims, Chris Sanders, Mike Olson, and others introduced

   _____ for snowboards.
10. Ski resort owners didn't allow snowboarding at first because they thought

    snowboarders _____.

ORDERING EVENTS

Number the sentences to show the correct order. Do this without looking at the passage. Then reread the passage to check your answers.

_____ Sherman Poppen invented the Snurfer for his children.

_____ Championship snowboarding competitions were held in Europe and America.

_____ Boys attached skate wheels to a small board.

_____ Snowboarding joined the Olympic Winter Games.

_____ Frank Nasworthy's invention allowed skateboarders to go fast and do tricks.

_____ Windsurfing became an Olympic sport.

_____ Drake and Schweitzer designed a way to attach a sail to a surfboard.

_____ Bill and Mark Richards got surfers interested in skateboarding.

 MAKING INFERENCES AND CONCLUDING

Information is not always stated directly in a passage. Sometimes we make guesses—inferences or conclusions—from the information that is in the reading. The answers to these questions are not directly stated in the passage. Circle the letter of the best answer.

1. From the passage, we can conclude that
   a. if it weren't for surfers, there wouldn't be skateboards.
   b. Nasworthy's invention made skateboarding possible.
   c. skateboarding owes its beginning to the imagination of children.

2. The writer seems to say that
   a. windsurfing didn't become popular until it was an Olympic sport.
   b. windsurfing is popular because it's more like sailing than surfing.
   c. people like windsurfing because it involves speed and daring.

3. We can infer from the passage that
   a. resort owners liked things as they were and were afraid to make changes.
   b. skiers and snowboarders will never be comfortable together on the slopes.
   c. resort owners were right in being worried about snowboarders.

DISCUSSION

Discuss the answers to the questions with your classmates.

1. Have you ever watched the X Games? Why?
2. Why do people like to watch extreme sports?
3. Why do people participate in extreme sports?
4. Do you think extreme sports are too dangerous and should be forbidden? Why?

WRITING

If you could choose to be a professional in any sport, what sport would it be? Write one or more paragraphs that tell about the sport, and explain why you chose it.

RESEARCH AND PRESENTATION

Find out where and how each of the following sports got started.

1. golf
2. gymnastics
3. ice skating
4. judo
5. mountain biking
6. pole vaulting
7. squash
8. surfing

Now work with a partner or small group. Choose one sport. Create a short presentation that tells where and how the sport originated and the names of people famous for the sport. Explain the sport, how it is played, and what equipment is needed. Be prepared to answer questions.

DID YOU KNOW . . . ?

In a sport called skysurfing, people jump out of airplanes with skateboards strapped to their feet!

Georgia O'Keeffe— Art Legend

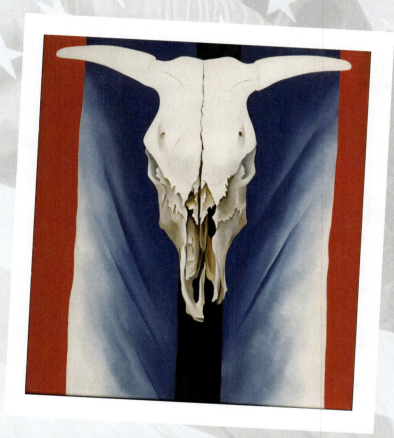

Georgia O'Keeffe, Cow's Skull: Red, White and Blue, *1949*.

PREREADING

Answer the questions.

1. What kind of paintings do you like?
2. Who are your favorite painters?
3. Who are some famous women painters you know?

Georgia O'Keeffe—Art Legend

1   In the 1930s, Georgia O'Keeffe was voted one of twelve outstanding living women, along with Eleanor Roosevelt and Helen Keller. By the 1960s, she was considered one of the greatest living artists. In the 1980s, she was still living and still painting. By then she had become an American legend.

2   Georgia O'Keeffe was born in 1887 in a Wisconsin farmhouse, the second of seven children. She was independent, **willful**, and she often **misbehaved**. She went places she was told not to go, like the **barnyard**. She did things she was told not to do, like eat dirt. She was sent to her room with only bread and milk for supper, but she only said, "I like bread and milk." Later in life, Georgia's life on the farm would influence her painting, such as when she painted parts of corn plants and flowers.

3   From the time she was nine, Georgia and her sisters were driven in a horse-drawn carriage to their art teacher's home. It was thought important in those days for young ladies to study art so they could decorate their homes. However, Georgia took her lessons more seriously. She had bigger plans for herself.

4   The O'Keeffes eventually moved off the farm to Williamsburg, Virginia. Georgia, with her love of the outdoors, was not happy there. She loved to swim and sail and fish, and unlike other southern girls, did not wear hats or gloves **to block** the sun. She was very unlike her classmates, who wore **frilly** dresses and spoke with southern accents. Georgia was a simple farm girl who dressed as plainly as she spoke. No matter how much her classmates tried to change her, she refused.

5   Within only a few weeks at her new school, Georgia was receiving special attention from Elizabeth May Willis, the headmistress and art instructor. She recognized O'Keeffe's talent and eventually became one of the many people who helped O'Keeffe during her life. In other areas, though, O'Keeffe behaved very badly. She fought with the girls and **disrupted** their studies. She taught others to play card games. She ate dirt, as she had as a child, and had **temper tantrums**. Once, she burned some of her drawings, saying that one day she would be famous and didn't want those pictures around when it happened.

6   O'Keeffe's belief that she could become a famous artist was rare among women of her time. It was accepted that women art students would become teachers. Actually, O'Keeffe did take a job as an art instructor after her studies in New York. First she was an instructor at a school in Amarillo, Texas, and then at West Texas State Normal College. While in Texas she began painting landscapes.* For the first

---

landscapes: pictures of country scenery, such as mountains, trees, and water

time she created art with a unique style, unlike anything she had been taught in school.

7   In 1918, she moved to New York, where her work was already starting to be noticed. In just a few years she was **praised** as the greatest woman artist of her time, the first woman artist to **excel** in America at a time when most artists were men. She painted in bright colors and a modern style, and every day became more famous, but she was still different. She wore men's clothes and long black dresses. She didn't talk much. When she did, she was often angry. It was the only way she knew how to express herself, other than through her art.

8   In 1924 she married Alfred Stieglitz, a famous photographer, twenty-four years older than O'Keeffe. The two great artists were very much in love but found life together very difficult. They often separated for long periods of time. He stayed in New York and she went to New Mexico, where she found inspiration for her work. After Stieglitz died in 1946, O'Keeffe moved to New Mexico permanently.

9   She lived in an **adobe** house in a tiny village called Abiquiu, at the end of 20 miles of dirt road. It had spectacular views of the New Mexico landscape, of the mountains and valleys, of sunrises and sunsets. It was here that Georgia O'Keeffe lived an isolated life for the next thirty years and produced her greatest works of art. She became the best-known American woman artist of the century, more famous than even she had ever imagined.

VOCABULARY

 MEANING

What is the meaning of the underlined words? Circle the letter of the correct answer. Use a dictionary to check your answers.

1. Georgia O'Keeffe was an independent and <u>willful</u> child.
   a. a person who is thoughtful of others
   b. a person who does what he or she likes in spite of other people
   c. a person who plans things in advance

2. She often <u>misbehaved</u>.
   a. did wrong or bad things
   b. said funny things
   c. got confused

3. She went to places she was told not to go, like the underlined barnyard.
   a. a yard near the railroad
   b. a building where tools are kept
   c. a yard on a farm with a fence around it

4. O'Keeffe did not wear hats or gloves to block the sun.
   a. to allow to enter or pass
   b. to add to or make stronger
   c. to stop from moving or doing

5. O'Keeffe did not wear frilly dresses or speak with a southern accent.
   a. with a lot of embroidery
   b. with a lot of gathered decorative edging
   c. colorful

6. Georgia O'Keeffe fought with the girls and disrupted their studies.
   a. interfered with
   b. controlled
   c. helped with

7. Georgia O'Keeffe had temper tantrums.
   a. loss of consciousness
   b. fits of anger
   c. periods of depression

8. O'Keeffe was praised as the greatest woman artist of her time.
   a. licensed
   b. recommended
   c. admired

9. She was the first woman artist to excel in America at a time when most artists were men.
   a. surpass
   b. be equal
   c. be inferior

10. O'Keeffe lived in an adobe house in a village in New Mexico.
    a. made of earth and straw
    b. made of stone
    c. made of wood

 USE

Work with a partner to answer the questions. Use complete sentences.

1. What are two *barnyard* animals?
2. What is something *willful* you did as a child?
3. Who is a woman who managed to *excel* in a field in which there were mostly men?
4. Other than New Mexico, where do people live in *adobe* houses?
5. What is something children do when they have *temper tantrums*?
6. Who has been *praised* as a great artist in your country?
7. What country has *frilly* dresses as a native costume?
8. What is something that people wear *to block* the sun?

COMPREHENSION

⭐ SKIMMING FOR MAIN IDEAS

Quickly read to find the main idea of each paragraph, and then circle the letter of the best answer.

1. Paragraph 1 is mainly about
   a. other outstanding women of Georgia O'Keeffe's time.
   b. Georgia O'Keeffe as an outstanding woman.
   c. Georgia O'Keeffe as a great artist of the 1960s.

2. The main topic of paragraph 7 is
   a. O'Keeffe's move to New York.
   b. O'Keeffe's personality and progress as an artist.
   c. O'Keeffe's choice of fashions and manner of speaking.

3. The main topic of paragraph 8 is
   a. Alfred Stieglitz's fame as a photographer.
   b. O'Keeffe's move to New Mexico.
   c. O'Keeffe's marriage to Stieglitz.

4. The last paragraph is mainly about
   a. where O'Keeffe lived and produced her greatest works of art.
   b. why O'Keeffe wanted to live an isolated life.
   c. what O'Keeffe's house was like in the village.

⭐ SCANNING FOR DETAILS

Reread the passage quickly to find key words and phrases from the questions. Circle _T_ if the sentence is true. Circle _F_ if the sentence is false.

1. When Georgia O'Keeffe was growing up, there were many famous women artists.   T   F
2. After moving to Texas, Georgia O'Keeffe developed her own unique style of art.   T   F
3. When Georgia was growing up, she was a quiet, well-behaved child.   T   F
4. Georgia O'Keeffe was born in 1887 in Wisconsin.   T   F
5. Georgia always got along well with her classmates.   T   F
6. O'Keeffe liked to use dark colors and a traditional style.   T   F

7. Georgia's early years on a farm influenced her painting
when she became an adult.   T   F
8. By the 1960s Georgia O'Keeffe was considered one of
the greatest living artists.   T   F
9. O'Keeffe's husband, Alfred Stieglitz, was a politician.   T   F
10. From the time she was a young girl, Georgia O'Keeffe
believed she would be famous.   T   F

 ORDERING EVENTS

Number the sentences to show the correct order. Do this without looking at the passage. Then reread the passage to check your answers.

_____ Georgia O'Keeffe moved to New York.

_____ Georgia and her sisters were driven to their art lessons in a horse-drawn carriage.

_____ Georgia O'Keeffe married Alfred Stieglitz.

_____ Elizabeth Willis recognized O'Keeffe's talent.

_____ O'Keeffe moved permanently to New Mexico.

_____ The O'Keeffe family moved to Williamsburg, Virginia.

_____ Georgia O'Keeffe was voted one of twelve outstanding living women.

_____ O'Keeffe taught art at West Texas State Normal College.

 MAKING INFERENCES AND CONCLUDING

Information is not always stated directly in a passage. Sometimes we make guesses—inferences or conclusions—from the information that is in the reading. The answers to these questions are not directly stated in the passage. Circle the letter of the best answer.

1. From the passage, we can conclude that
   a. Georgia O'Keeffe had a unique personality all of her life.
   b. O'Keeffe led a very traditional way of life.
   c. O'Keeffe's talent didn't show until she studied in New York.

2. We can infer from the passage that
   a. when O'Keeffe was raised, women were not trained for careers.
   b. O'Keeffe was famous for only a brief period in her life.
   c. Stieglitz and O'Keeffe had a happy and contented life together.

3. The writer seems to say that
   a. what influenced Georgia O'Keeffe's art style the most was her training.
   b. O'Keeffe was a friendly woman who liked to be around people.
   c. O'Keeffe expressed her thoughts and emotions through her art.

DISCUSSION

Discuss the answers to the questions with your classmates.

1. Who are some famous artists who are unusual and live strange lives? Is this true of most artists? Why?
2. Abstract art can sometimes be a spot of paint on a canvas. Some people think this is not true art. What do you think?
3. Is painting a gift you are born with or is it learned? Why?
4. What were some of Georgia O'Keeffe's personality traits? How do you think they helped her to become a famous artist?

WRITING

Write one or more paragraphs about an art style you like. Be sure to give reasons and examples.

RESEARCH AND PRESENTATION

Find two artists who are famous for each style of modern art.

1. cubism
2. expressionism
3. fauvism
4. impressionism
5. pop art
6. surrealism

Now work with a partner or small group. Prepare a biography of one famous artist for your class. Include photos of the artist's works and a description of his or her style. Be prepared to answer questions.

DID YOU KNOW . . . ?
Many artists are left-handed, including such famous artists as Leonardo da Vinci, Michelangelo, Raphael, and Rembrandt.

The Last Queen of Hawaii

PREREADING

Answer the questions.

1. Where is Hawaii located?
2. What are some customs of the native Hawaiians?
3. Why do tourists like to go to Hawaii?

The Last Queen of Hawaii

1   In 1810, the famous chief Kamehameha brought all the Hawaiian islands together. Under the leadership of King Kamehameha I, Hawaii was peaceful and **prosperous**. But by the time of his death in 1819, things were already changing. Foreigners had come to the islands. They were sailors, traders, and missionaries. Missionaries go to a country to teach and spread religion there. Foreigners often bring diseases that sicken and kill many natives. All these foreigners brought new ways of life, new diseases, and new religions. They became very powerful. Some of the Hawaiians didn't like the changes the foreigners were making. They tried to stop them, but they couldn't. In 1838, during this time of troubles, Lydia Kamakaeha was born. She would someday be the last ruler of the Hawaiian kingdom.

2   Lydia was the third of ten children born to two Hawaiian high chiefs. Her parents did not bring her up, however. There was a custom in Hawaii at that time that children were given to other families. This custom made friendships and kept peace among tribes. After Lydia was born, she was **adopted by** another chief and his wife. Other chiefs also adopted most of Lydia's brothers and sisters. For this reason, they rarely saw each other and were never close.

3   Lydia went to a special school for the children of high chiefs. It was **run by** the missionaries. Lydia was an intelligent girl and a good student. She was also a talented poet and musician. During the time Lydia was growing up, the foreigners were taking over the islands. They ran the schools, churches, and hospitals. They were in shipping, farming, ranching, and trade. They were a big part of the government. Many of them were Americans. They started talking about annexation—they wanted the United States to take control of Hawaii and make it a territory. Lydia did not like what these people were doing and saying.

4   At age twenty-four, Lydia married John Dominis, a man from Boston. Lydia's brother, David Kalakaua became king in 1874. In 1877, his younger brother died, and Lydia became the next in line to the throne.* She became known by her royal name, Liliuokalani, which means "salt air of heaven." Liliuokalani began to prepare for her future. She went to **social events** in the palace. She visited all the islands and talked to the people. She went to England to meet Queen Victoria. She traveled to the United States to meet President Grover Cleveland. Liliuokalani was proud to be Hawaiian. She loved her people, and she was unhappy about the power of the foreigners. She believed that Hawaii belonged to the native Hawaiians.

---

*throne: the rank, office, and power given to a king or queen

5   In 1887, Liliuokalani went to England. While she was gone, the Americans forced King Kalakaua to agree to a new constitution.** The new constitution took almost all power away from the king. It gave the power to the people in government, who were mostly Americans. They took top government jobs from native Hawaiians and gave them to Americans.

6   Four years later, in 1891, when King Kalakaua died, Liliuokalani became queen. Liliuokalani did not want American businessmen to run Hawaii. She tried to put in a new constitution. It took power and rights away from the foreigners and gave them back to the native Hawaiians. It also returned power to the throne. The Americans living in Hawaii acted quickly. They took over official government buildings. They called in American **troops** to protect themselves and the property they owned. They forced Queen Liliuokalani to **give up** her throne. They asked President Cleveland to annex Hawaii, but when he refused, they **set up** their own government. They named a lawyer, Sanford Dole, as the new president.

7   Liliuokalani asked President Cleveland to give her back her throne. She waited and waited for the government to help her. She told the Hawaiian people not to fight. She told them to be calm and patient. She believed that the U.S. government would not allow this terrible thing to happen. Meanwhile, the Americans in Hawaii refused to give up their control. In the end, President Cleveland was not willing to use force against them.

8   In January of 1895, a group of Hawaiians tried to fight against the new government, but they were unsuccessful. Liliuokalani **was arrested**. The **authorities** said that she had planned the revolt. They told her that she must give up her throne or all her supporters would be killed. On January 24, she gave up her title as Hawaii's queen. She was brought to **trial**. Her punishment was $5,000 and five years of hard labor,*** but this never happened. Instead, Liliuokalani was put in a room alone for nine months. She had no visitors. She wrote books, poems, and music. She wrote a song called "Aloha Oe" (Farewell to Thee), which became world famous.

9   In 1896, Hawaiian President Dole let Liliuokalani go free. She traveled to Boston to see her husband's family. She also went to Washington, D.C., to thank President Cleveland for not annexing Hawaii. She still had hopes of returning to her place as the leader of her people.

10   Two years later, a new U.S. president, William McKinley, made Hawaii an official territory of the United States. Liliuokalani did not go to the ceremony in Honolulu. Her hopes were gone. She spent the rest of her days living quietly with her writing and music. Her people loved her dearly until her death in 1917. In 1959, Hawaii became the fiftieth state of the United States.

** *constitution:* a country's written laws
****hard labor:* hard work that prisoners are forced to do

VOCABULARY

 MEANING

Complete each definition with one of the following. Guess your answers, and then check them with a dictionary.

prosperous	run by	troops	set up	authorities
adopted by	social events	give up	was arrested	trial

1. Members of an army are soldiers, or _____ .

2. If you _____ something, you stop having or doing it.

3. A person _____ if he or she was taken to jail in the name of the law.

4. Parties and other occasions when people get together are

   _____ .

5. To _____ a business or organization means to start or establish it.

6. A _____ is a process of hearing and judging a person or case in a court of law.

7. People with the power or right to control and command others are

   _____ .

8. To be _____ someone is to have them take you into their family and be parents to you.

9. When an institution or business is controlled and operated by someone, or a group of people, it is _____ them.

10. When people are _____ , they have everything they need to live happy and comfortable lives.

 USE

Work with a partner to answer the questions. Use complete sentences.

1. What are some *social events* that families have in your country?
2. Who are the *authorities* in a school or university?
3. What are some of the things that happen during a *trial*?
4. What are some of the responsibilities of the *troops* in a country?
5. What are some things that people have when they are *prosperous*?

6. What are some institutions that are *run by* the government in your country?

7. What are the advantages of being *adopted by* a family?

8. What are some things a person must do in order to *set up* a new business?

COMPREHENSION

 ### SKIMMING FOR MAIN IDEAS

Quickly read to find the main idea of each paragraph, and then circle the letter of the best answer.

1. Paragraph 1 is mainly about
   a. what King Kamehameha did for his people.
   b. the changes brought to Hawaii by foreigners.
   c. the importance of Lydia Kamakaeha's birth.

2. The main topic of paragraph 4 is
   a. how Liliuokalani prepared to be queen.
   b. what social events Liliuokalani attended.
   c. what kind of king Kalakaua was for Hawaii.

3. The main topic of paragraph 6 is
   a. how Liliuokalani felt about the Americans.
   b. how the Americans took power in Hawaii.
   c. how Liliuokalani tried to gain more power.

4. Paragraph 8 is mainly about
   a. how the Hawaiians tried to fight the new government.
   b. why Liliuokalani gave up her throne.
   c. what the new government did to Queen Liliuokalani.

 ### SCANNING FOR DETAILS

Reread the passage quickly to find key words and phrases from the questions. Then circle the letter of the correct answer.

1. Lydia Kamakaeha was born during a time of
   a. calm and plenty.
   b. troubles.
   c. war.

2. Lydia was adopted because
   a. it was a custom in her country.
   b. her parents had died.
   c. the missionaries wanted it.

3. Lydia went to a special school for
   a. American children.
   b. children with talent for poetry and music.
   c. children of Hawaiian chiefs.

4. The name Liliuokalani means
   a. salt air of heaven.
   b. queen of the ocean.
   c. flower of the islands.

5. While Liliuokalani was in England,
   a. her brother died.
   b. the Americans set up their own government.
   c. King Kalakaua lost much of his power.

6. Liliuokalani wanted the islands of Hawaii to
   a. become a territory of the United States.
   b. be governed by native Hawaiians.
   c. be divided into separate countries.

7. Liliuokalani told the Hawaiian people to
   a. fight the Americans.
   b. set up their own businesses.
   c. be calm and not make trouble.

8. After Liliuokalani's trial, the authorities made her
   a. work at hard labor for five years.
   b. stay alone in a room for nine months.
   c. write books about Hawaii.

9. In 1896, Liliuokalani traveled to Boston to visit
   a. her husband's family.
   b. important lawyers and government officials.
   c. President Cleveland.

10. Hawaii became a state of the United States in
    a. 1895.
    b. 1917.
    c. 1959.

★ ORDERING EVENTS

Number the sentences to show the correct order. Do this without looking at the passage. Then reread the passage to check your answers.

_____ Lydia Kamakaeha was born.

_____ Americans forced Queen Liliuokalani to give up her throne.

_____ Foreigners began building businesses and became powerful.

_____ King Kamehameha united the Hawaiian Islands.

_____ Americans forced a new constitution on King Kalakaua.

_____ Traders, missionaries, and other outsiders brought changes to the islands.

⭐ MAKING INFERENCES AND CONCLUDING

Information is not always stated directly in a passage. Sometimes we make guesses—inferences or conclusions—from the information that is in the reading. The answers to these questions are not directly stated in the passage. Circle the letter of the best answer.

1. From the passage, we can conclude that
   a. Kamehameha was not a good king for Hawaii.
   b. David Kalakaua was a strong king who defended the Hawaiian people.
   c. Queen Liliuokalani was a strong, brave leader.

2. We can infer from the passage that the foreigners
   a. wanted to protect their own interests.
   b. wanted what was best for the Hawaiians.
   c. made life better for everyone on the islands.

3. The writer seems to say that Liliuokalani
   a. wanted the Hawaiians to fight the Americans.
   b. was eventually happy that the Americans took power.
   c. always felt sorry about the American takeover of Hawaii.

DISCUSSION

Discuss the answers to the questions with your classmates.

1. Do you think America was right to make Hawaii a territory? Why?
2. Do you think other countries were interested in taking over Hawaii, too? Why would other countries want control over Hawaii?
3. What other country do you know that was taken over by foreigners? Did it make the country worse or better? Why?
4. What is your opinion of Queen Liliuokalani?

WRITING

Would you like to live on an island like Hawaii? Write one or more paragraphs that give reasons why.

RESEARCH AND PRESENTATION

Find out the following facts about the state of Hawaii.

1. The state capitol
2. How the islands were formed
3. The largest and smallest islands
4. The youngest and oldest islands
5. The climate
6. Which volcano is still erupting today
7. Traditional Hawaiian dress, music, and dance
8. Three activities for tourists on the islands

Now work with a partner or small group. Create a travel poster for Hawaii with a map of the important islands and what is special about each one. Present the poster to your class. Be ready to answer questions about it from your classmates.

DID YOU KNOW . . . ?

The wettest place in the United States is Mount Waialeale on the Hawaiian island of Kauai, where the average rainfall is almost 40 feet a year!

Alaska—the Last Frontier

PREREADING

Answer the questions.

1. Look at the picture of this animal. In what parts of the world is it found?
2. What do you know about Alaska?
3. Would you like to live there? Why?

Alaska—the Last Frontier

1   Alaska became the forty-ninth state in January 1959. There is nothing small or ordinary about Alaska. It is America's largest state. It has the highest mountain and the largest glacier in North America. Its chain of volcanoes is the longest in the world. It has **vast** regions of uninhabited land richly diverse in both geography and wildlife. It is a remarkable place known as the "Last Frontier."

2   Alaska fits its name very well. It comes from the word *alyeska*, meaning "Great Land" in the language of its native Aleut people. Alaska covers 591,004 square miles. Rhode Island would fit into Alaska 480 times! The highest point in Alaska is 20,320-foot Mount McKinley. The sixteen highest mountains in the United States are all in Alaska. There are also about 100,000 glaciers. The largest, Malaspina Glacier, covers 850 square miles. Alaska also has more than 3 million lakes and 3,000 rivers, much more than any other state.

3   Everything about Alaska seems big. The largest salmon **on record** was caught in 1985 in Alaska's Kenia River. It weighed 97 pounds, 4 ounces. Alaska's brown bears, Kodiak bears, are the world's largest bears. Even the vegetables grown there are big. Cabbages have been known to weigh 95 pounds, and carrots to be 3 feet long! If you took a trip through Alaska, it would take quite a long while to cover its vast territory. You'd have to take an airplane from place to place because much of Alaska doesn't have roads.

4   Along the coast you would see thousands of islands, rocks, and **reefs**. You'd see glaciers and icebergs, which are huge pieces of glaciers that fall into the water. Glaciers cover nearly 29,000 square miles of Alaska. Most are in the south and southeast.

5   In south-central Alaska, you'd fly over the Alaskan **Mountain Range** and Mount McKinley. Thousands of visitors have climbed up Mount McKinley. Others have died trying. The youngest person to climb Mount McKinley was Taras Genet of Talkeetna, Alaska, who climbed it in 1991 when he was twelve years old.

6   No doubt you would visit several of Alaska's national parks. In these protected lands there are glaciers, mountains, active volcanoes, lakes, rivers, forests, and wildlife of many kinds. Besides Kodiak bears, there are grizzly bears, polar bears, moose, caribou, wolves, porcupines, beavers, mountain goats, foxes, and squirrels. Alaska has 450 kinds of birds. In its waters, whales and dolphins swim along the coast. Seals, walruses, and sea otters are also found there.

7   Part of Alaska lies within the Arctic Circle. The land there is called *tundra*. There are no trees because the soil is always frozen. This frozen soil, called *permafrost*, **thaws** on the surface during the summer, when it

is covered with a thick layer of **mosses**, wildflowers, and grasses. People who live there have a special problem because of the permafrost. A house built on it sometimes causes it to thaw beneath the house. The thawed soil begins to sink down, and the house goes with it! Many arctic inhabitants build their houses on platforms so they can be moved from time to time.

8   If you lived in the arctic, you would know why Alaska is also called the "Land of the Midnight Sun." At Barrow, the northernmost point, the sun does not set from May 10 to August 2. There is daylight all that time. Then from November 18 to January 24, Barrow has no sunlight. The average temperature is minus 11 degrees Fahrenheit. If you went to the arctic in the spring and autumn, you'd see the northern lights. This is a **natural phenomenon** in which the night skies are filled with **spectacular** colors, also called the aurora borealis.

9   Alaska is a very different and special place, and so are its people. Alaska has a very small population for such a big place. Many Alaskan towns have fewer than 100 residents. One such town is Chicken, which has a population of thirty-seven. Many towns, like Chicken, have unusual names, such as Clam Gulch, Candle, Beaver, Deadhorse, King Salmon, and Eek. Many were named by the adventurous and often **eccentric** prospectors who came to Alaska looking for gold in the 1800s. In 1900, another kind of valuable substance was found—oil—and the first well was drilled.

10   Most Alaskans live in the cities, such as Anchorage, Fairbanks, and Juneau, where there is work and a modern way of life. The population of Alaska is growing rapidly, and today about two-thirds of Alaskans were born in other places. They come from many countries to work in the oil, mining, **timber**, and fishing industries.

11   Native-born Alaskans include both native peoples and the descendants of the early settlers. The natives—the Eskimos, Aleuts, and Indians— migrated to Alaska from Siberia as far back as 15,000 years ago. Some of the natives still live the way their ancestors did, hunting and fishing in the wilderness. Others have modern lives in the cities. However, no matter where they live, when they got there, or what ethnic group they belong to, all Alaskans have one thing in common: the splendors of the great land in which they live.

VOCABULARY

 MEANING

Complete each definition with one of the following. Guess your answers, and then check them with a dictionary.

vast	reefs	thaws	natural phenomenon	eccentric
on record	mountain range	mosses	spectacular	timber

1. _____ is wood or trees grown for use in building.

2. People who are strange and behave in an unusual manner are _____.

3. Facts or events _____ are written down and preserved.

4. Something great in size is _____.

5. _____ are lines of rocks or sand near the surface of the sea.

6. When something frozen becomes soft or liquid, it _____.

7. _____ are small, flat, green or yellow plants without flowers that grow like a thin carpet on wet soil.

8. A connected line or chain of mountains is a _____.

9. Something _____ is impressive and dramatic to watch.

10. An unusual event in nature is a _____.

 USE

Work with a partner to answer the questions. Use complete sentences.

1. Where do *mosses* usually grow?
2. What is a country that has *vast* areas of wilderness?
3. What is the name of one of the most famous *reefs* in the world?
4. What is a *spectacular* area of your country?
5. What *natural phenomenon* would you like to see?
6. Who is a famous person who is also known as *eccentric*?
7. What is the name of a well-known *mountain range* in your country or in the world?
8. What kind of *timber* is used for making furniture in your country?

COMPREHENSION

 SKIMMING FOR MAIN IDEAS

Quickly read to find the main idea of each paragraph, and then circle the letter of the best answer.

1. Paragraph 3 is mainly about the fact that
   a. Alaska covers a vast area.
   b. everything in Alaska is big.
   c. vegetables that grow in Alaska are big.

2. Paragraph 7 is mainly about
   a. the characteristics of the tundra.
   b. when summer comes to the tundra.
   c. the people who live in the tundra.

3. Paragraph 8 mostly discusses the fact that
   a. spring is the best time to visit Alaska.
   b. the northern lights are a natural phenomenon.
   c. Alaska is known as the "Land of the Midnight Sun."

4. The last paragraph is mainly about
   a. native peoples and descendants of the early settlers who make up the native-born Alaskans.
   b. the native peoples who still live the way their ancestors did.
   c. native-born Alaskans who live in big cities today.

⭐ **SCANNING FOR DETAILS**

Reread the passage quickly to find key words and phrases from the questions. Then write the correct answer on the line.

1. Alaska means _____ in the language of its native _____ people.

2. Alaska's brown bears, called _____ bears, are the largest bears in the world.

3. The treeless land within the Arctic Circle is called _____.

4. Because the sun does not set during summer in the northernmost regions, Alaska is also called _____.

5. Native-born Alaskans include both _____ and _____.

6. The highest point in Alaska is _____, which is _____ feet high.

7. The colors that can be seen in the night skies in autumn are called the _____ or _____.

8. In Alaska there are about _____ glaciers, 3 million lakes, and _____ rivers.

9. The best way to travel across Alaska is by _____ because _____.

10. The native people of Alaska migrated from _____.

⭐ ORDERING EVENTS

Number the sentences to show the correct order. Do this without looking at the passage. Then reread the passage to check your answers.

_____ Taras Genet climbed Mount McKinley.

_____ Prospectors came to Alaska looking for gold.

_____ Eskimos, Aleuts, and Indians migrated to Alaska.

_____ Alaska became a state.

_____ The largest salmon on record was caught in the Kenia River.

_____ The first oil well was drilled.

⭐ MAKING INFERENCES AND CONCLUDING

Information is not always stated directly in a passage. Sometimes we make guesses—inferences or conclusions—from the information that is in the reading. The answers to these questions are not directly stated in the passage. Circle the letter of the best answer.

1. From the passage, we can conclude that
   a. all Alaskans travel by plane.
   b. traveling through Alaska on foot would be difficult and dangerous.
   c. because most of Alaska is wilderness, there isn't much for visitors to see there.

2. We can infer from the passage that
   a. it is impossible for people to live in the area within the Arctic Circle.
   b. the native Alaskans have lost their ability to survive in the wilderness.
   c. the majority of Alaska's population are immigrants living in urban areas.

3. The writer seems to say that
   a. people who live in Alaska must learn to live in the wilderness.
   b. Alaska's native people adapted to the harsh climate and made use of natural resources.
   c. most people who went to Alaska looking for gold didn't stay.

DISCUSSION

Discuss the answers to the questions with your classmates.

1. Some people in Alaska live alone in the wilderness. What are the pros and cons of living this way?
2. Do you believe that native peoples should leave their traditional ways of life and live in a modern society? Why?
3. What area of your country is considered very beautiful? How is it similar to or different from Alaska?
4. What is your favorite climate to live in? Why? How do you think climate affects the way people live?

WRITING

Think about two different types of houses that are found in different environments. Write one paragraph about how the houses are the same and another paragraph about how they are different. Explain how the building materials and styles are meant to adapt to each environment.

RESEARCH AND PRESENTATION

Find the following facts about Alaska.

1. animals
2. festivals
3. fishing
4. national parks
5. plants
6. population

Now work with a partner or small group. Pick one topic and prepare a presentation for your class. Be prepared to answer questions.

DID YOU KNOW . . . ?

A polar bear's wide paws have a thick, rough skin under them that helps the bears travel over snow and ice without slipping.

Susan Butcher on the Iditarod Trail

Answer the questions.

1. Look at the picture. What is this sport? Where does it take place?
2. Do you think this sport is dangerous? Why?
3. What other snow sports do you know?

Susan Butcher on the Iditarod Trail

1   It was 1982, and an hour into the race, Susan Butcher and her **sled dog team** sped down a hill, **skidded off** the trail, and crashed into a fallen tree. With a hurt shoulder, Susan **untangled** her sled and team of Alaskan husky dogs and continued the **grueling** race across the frozen Alaskan wilderness. It was the fourth year she had run this race, known as the Iditarod, and she wanted very much to win it.

2   The history of the Iditarod goes back to 1925 when a doctor in Nome, Alaska, was **desperately** in need of medicine to stop the spread of a deadly disease called diphtheria. Only a hospital in Anchorage, 700 miles away, had the supplies he needed. But it was January, too dangerous a time to send a boat across the frozen Bering Sea and too stormy for his tiny airplane. The only hope was to use sled dog teams following an old native **trail** through the mountains and tundra. The medicine was passed from one man and his sled team to another along the trail. It was named Iditarod after one of the towns it passed through. Storms of wind and snow and temperatures as cold as 60 degrees below zero did not stop them, and the medicine was delivered in record time. Most of the Iditarod Trail Sled Dog Race follows the route of the famous medicine run. It is over 1,000 miles long and is considered the toughest race in the world. In 1978, Susan Butcher entered it for the first time.

3   Susan Butcher was born in 1954 in Cambridge, Massachusetts, and had a love of animals and the outdoors from the time she was a child. She was athletic and loved to sail. She often imagined herself sailing around the world by herself. Little did she know what she would really do in her life. In her teens Susan was given a Siberian husky dog and became very interested in the history of huskies as sled dogs. At the age of seventeen she moved to Colorado where she began to train and run dogs for a racing **kennel**. After reading about the Iditarod race in a magazine, Susan moved to Alaska. She worked at several jobs to earn enough money to buy herself a sled and team of huskies. Susan achieved her dream of being in the Iditarod after years of hard work and **rigorous** training.

4   In her first race in 1978 she finished nineteenth and became the first woman to finish in the top twenty. The following year she finished ninth, and the third year in fifth place. In her fourth race in 1982, she came in second. The next year she again finished in the top twenty. In 1984, she was leading her team across a frozen waterway when suddenly the ice began to shake and fall apart. Susan and her team fell into the **frigid** water. Her lead dog managed to get to shore and pulled Susan and the other dogs out of danger. Susan's clothes were soaked and already starting

to freeze. Nevertheless she kept going, running for a while to dry her clothes, and then riding the sled so her lungs wouldn't freeze from her heavy breathing. Remarkably, she pulled into Nome in second place.

5   In 1985, many people thought Susan would win. However, it was not to be. On the trail, she met a starving moose, a very large hoofed animal similar to a deer, that attacked her dogs, killing two and injuring eleven. Susan had to leave the race. That year, it was another woman, Libby Riddles of Teller, Alaska, who became the first woman to win the Iditarod. In 1986, Susan joined the race again. This time her lead dogs fell off a shelf of ice. Susan managed to rescue them and kept going through blinding snowstorms. Sometimes she was so tired she began to imagine things, such as a forest where there was none. More than once she lost the snow-covered trail. But others did, too, and Susan won the race. She won again in 1987. In 1988, she became the first ever to win three Iditarod races in a row.* Unbelievably, Susan became a winner for the fourth time in 1990. Her strength, **stamina**, and dedication had made her the most famous dog sled racer in the world.

6   Susan Butcher died at the age of fifty-one on August 5, 2006, from leukemia. She left behind a husband, two daughters, and a life of great accomplishment. Susan took part in over seventeen races between 1978 and 1994. She won four Iditarod championships, and twelve times she placed in the top five. She introduced a new method of dog training and helped change the way the race was run. Today she remains the most famous professional athlete in Alaskan state history.

---

*in a row: one right after the other

VOCABULARY

 MEANING

Complete each definition with one of the following. Guess your answers, and then check them with a dictionary.

sled dog team	untangled	desperately	kennel	frigid
skidded off	grueling	trail	rigorous	stamina

1. A person with _____ has a strong body or mind to fight tiredness and keep on going.

2. Extremely cold is _____.

3. A place where dogs are kept is a _____.

4. A group of dogs working together to pull a small vehicle for sliding along snow is a _____.

5. If a vehicle _____ the road, it would have slipped sideways out of control.

6. Exercise that demands a lot of force and energy is _____.

7. A path across rough or wild country is a _____.

8. Something that is very hard and exhausting is _____.

9. When something is _____, the twisted parts are made free.

10. To suffer from extreme need of something is to need it _____.

 ## USE

Work with a partner to answer the questions. Use complete sentences.

1. What is a *grueling* sport in your country?
2. What is one animal that is often used to make a *trail* through wilderness?
3. What are two things that dogs need in a *kennel*?
4. What is an activity that requires *rigorous* training?
5. Besides Alaska, what is a *frigid* part of the world?
6. How is *stamina* different from strength?
7. What group of people in your country or the world is *desperately* in need of help?
8. What is something that often needs to be *untangled*?

COMPREHENSION

 ### SKIMMING FOR MAIN IDEAS

Quickly read to find the main idea of each paragraph, and then circle the letter of the best answer.

1. Paragraph 2 is mainly about
   a. the history behind the Iditarod race.
   b. the difficulty of transportation in Alaska.
   c. the suffering of the people in Nome, Alaska.

2. The main topic of paragraph 3 is
   a. Susan Butcher's move to Colorado.
   b. Susan Butcher's life up to the time of her first Iditarod race.
   c. Susan Butcher's love of dogs and her work with them in Colorado.

3. The main topic of paragraph 4 is
    a. Susan Butcher's historical win in 1978.
    b. Susan Butcher's accident on the trail in 1984.
    c. Susan Butcher's top twenty finishes in spite of all odds.
4. Paragraph 5 is mainly about
    a. Susan Butcher's courage and determination leading to her success.
    b. Susan Butcher meeting disaster and being forced to leave the 1985 race.
    c. Libby Riddles becoming the first woman to win the Iditarod.

 SCANNING FOR DETAILS

Reread the passage quickly to find key words and phrases from the questions. Each sentence has an incorrect fact. Cross out the incorrect fact, and write the correct answer above it.

1. The Iditarod Trail Sled Dog Race is over 3,000 miles long.

2. The history of the Iditarod began in 1940 when a doctor in Nome, Alaska, was desperately in need of medicine.

3. At seventeen, Susan Butcher moved to Colorado and went to college to become a veterinarian.

4. In her first Iditarod race, Susan Butcher became the first woman to finish in the top ten.

5. A plane couldn't be used to get the necessary medicine because they couldn't find a pilot.

6. In 1985, Susan left the race after a bear attacked her dogs.

7. In 1987, Susan Butcher became the first person ever to win three Iditarod races in a row.

8. Susan Butcher moved to Alaska after someone offered her a job.

9. In 1984, even after falling into freezing cold water, Susan Butcher continued the race and came in first.

10. The Iditarod trail is named after the doctor who sent for the medicine.

⭐ ORDERING EVENTS

Number the sentences to show the correct order. Do this without looking at the passage. Then reread the passage to check your answers.

_____ Susan Butcher moved to Colorado and began training dogs.

_____ Susan Butcher moved to Alaska.

_____ Medicine was carried along the difficult and dangerous Iditarod trail.

_____ People were in danger of getting the deadly diphtheria disease.

_____ Susan Butcher entered her first Iditarod race.

_____ Susan was given a Siberian husky dog.

_____ Susan Butcher read about the Iditarod race.

MAKING INFERENCES AND CONCLUDING

Information is not always stated directly in a passage. Sometimes we make guesses—inferences or conclusions—from the information that is in the reading. The answers to these questions are not directly stated in the passage. Circle the letter of the best answer.

1. From the passage, we can conclude that
   a. Susan Butcher could probably have won the Iditarod when she was still in her teens.
   b. it takes years of training to be able to win an Iditarod race.
   c. the Iditarod race is the kind of athletic event that almost anyone can enter and have a chance to win.

2. We can infer from the passage that
   a. the courage of the men and their sled teams saved Nome's people.
   b. other forms of transportation would have been more successful than the sled teams in bringing medicine to Nome.
   c. by the time the medicine arrived from Anchorage, it was too late.

3. The writer seems to say that
   a. Susan Butcher achieved success as a result of courage, hard work, and determination.
   b. the 1984 Iditarod was an easy race for Susan Butcher to win.
   c. Susan Butcher was famous before she participated in Iditarod races.

DISCUSSION

Discuss the answers to the questions with your classmates.

1. Why do some people risk their lives at a sport?
2. What other sports involve animals?
3. Do you think men and women should compete against each other in a sport? Why?
4. What other winter sports heroes do you know? What are they famous for?

WRITING

Choose a popular or special sport that is played in your country. Write one or more paragraphs that describe when and how the game is played and why it is popular.

RESEARCH AND DISCUSSION

Look up the following dangerous sports. Find out what dangers are involved in each.

1. cliff diving
2. extreme skiing
3. free running
4. hang gliding
5. rock climbing
6. skydiving

Now work with a partner or small group. Choose one of the sports, and prepare a short presentation about it. Explain what it is, how it started, and what makes it dangerous. Provide pictures. Be prepared to answer questions.

DID YOU KNOW . . . ?

Alaskan malamutes are the largest, strongest, and oldest sled dogs native to North America. They have such strong wills that on the trail they will sometimes work to death for their masters.

A Perfect Lunar Landing

PREREADING

Answer the questions.

1. Would you like to go to the moon? Why?
2. Which other planet would you like to visit? Why?
3. Would you like to live in a space station? Why?

A Perfect Lunar Landing

1   On July 16, 1969, after traveling 239,000 miles into space, the *Apollo 11* spacecraft slowly circled around the moon. Attached to it was the *Eagle*, a smaller spacecraft called a **lunar** module. With two astronauts aboard, it separated from the *Apollo 11*. It **drifted** downward and landed without a splash on the moon's Sea of Tranquility. Then one of the most memorable moments in American and scientific history occurred. Neil Armstrong, dressed in a white spacesuit, stepped down from his spacecraft onto the moon. He became the first human being to **set foot in** another world. He said the historic words, "One small step for man; one giant leap for mankind."

2   Neil was soon joined by Buzz Aldrin, and together they explored the moon on foot. It was a very different world from our own. On the moon there is no air, water, or weather. Since sound travels on air, there is only silence. There are no living things. The ground is **barren** and is covered with gray rock and gray, powder-like soil. The daytime temperature is hot enough to boil water at 212 degrees Fahrenheit. At night, water would freeze instantly because the temperature drops to about 280 degrees below zero. There is no water on the moon, however. It is drier than any desert on Earth.

3   There are large dark areas on the moon that are hundreds of miles across. They are made from rock inside the moon that melted, flowed out, and flooded the lowlands. An Italian astronomer named Giovanni Riccioli used a telescope to map the moon 350 years ago. He thought the smooth, dark areas were seas. Although we know better now, we still call these areas seas, like the Sea of Tranquility. That's where Aldrin and Armstrong walked, picked up samples of rock and soil, set up experiments, and took photographs. They even enjoyed themselves by taking great leaps, jumping farther than even the greatest athlete due to the much weaker **gravity** on the moon. Overweight people would like it on the moon because you weigh six times less there than you weigh on Earth. The astronauts spent a total of two and a half hours on the moon's surface. When they returned to *Apollo 11*, they left behind a plaque that said, "Here men from the planet earth first set foot upon the moon, July 1969, A.D. We came in peace for all mankind."

4   Five more landings were made on the moon over the next three and a half years. Ten more astronauts became "moon walkers." They explored various regions from the flat "seas" to the **rugged** highlands. On the last three missions, they were able to cover more territory because they had a vehicle called a lunar rover, or "moon buggy." It was **collapsible**. It was powered by electric motors and was able to carry two astronauts and their equipment at a top speed of 9 miles an hour.

5   *Apollo 17* was the last spacecraft to take men to the moon in December 1972. Altogether there were six successful landings by *Apollo 11*, *12*, *14*, *15*, *16*, and *17*; unlucky *Apollo 13* was damaged by an explosion on the way to the moon. The crew had to use their lunar module to make it safely back to Earth.

6   Today the United States, in cooperation with other countries, is working on a new space exploration program. The goal is to return to the moon and build a moon base. Scientific laboratories and observatories will be built, as well as **living quarters**. There will be lunar **ferries** that will travel to the moon and back with scientists and engineers aboard. Soon a new generation of interplanetary **craft** will be built to carry explorers to Mars and afterward to other planets in our universe. We are in a new era of spaceflight that will take us to the farthest reaches of science and exploration.

VOCABULARY

 MEANING

Complete each definition with one of the following. Guess your answers, and then check them with a dictionary.

lunar	set foot in	gravity	collapsible	ferries
drifted	barren	rugged	living quarters	craft

1. If something is _____ it can be bent or folded to make it smaller.

2. Something that is of, to, or for the moon is called _____.

3. The places or areas where people live are _____.

4. _____ is the natural force by which objects are attracted to each other.

5. Land that is _____ is not productive and has nothing on it.

6. To _____ a place is to visit or enter it.

7. _____ take people or things across a sea or continent in an organized service or route.

8. Land that is _____ is rough and uneven.

9. A vessel or a ship that travels through the air or in the sea is a _____.

10. _____ means floated or moved by water or the wind.

USE

Work with a partner to answer the questions. Use complete sentences.

1. Where is there a *rugged* area in your country?
2. Why are *collapsible* objects very useful?
3. What are some characteristics of *ferries*?
4. What is one type of *craft* used to travel into space today?
5. What happens during a *lunar* eclipse?
6. What do you think the lunar *living quarters* will be like?
7. What is a *barren* area in your country or in the world?
8. Who is a famous explorer who *set foot in* previously unexplored lands?

COMPREHENSION

 SKIMMING FOR MAIN IDEAS

Quickly read to find the main idea of each paragraph, and then circle the letter of the best answer.

1. The main topic of paragraph 1 is
   a. how man first landed on the moon.
   b. what a lunar module is.
   c. the job of Neil Armstrong on the moon.

2. Paragraph 2 is mainly about
   a. how Neil Armstrong and Buzz Aldrin explored the moon.
   b. the temperature of the moon.
   c. the characteristics of the moon.

3. The main topic of paragraph 4 is
   a. collapsible moon buggies.
   b. the five other landings on the moon.
   c. the astronauts who walked on the moon.

4. The last paragraph is mainly about the fact that
   a. a moon base is expected in the next century.
   b. there are plans for future space travel and living.
   c. ferries will travel to the moon from Earth.

Reread the passage quickly to find key words and phrases from the questions. Then write the correct answer on the line.

1. An Italian astronomer by the name of _____ used a _____ to map the moon 350 years ago.

2. On the last three moon missions, the astronauts used a _____, or "_____," to travel on the surface of the moon.

3. On the first lunar landing, the *Eagle* landed on an area of the moon called _____.

4. The last spacecraft to take men to the moon in December 1972 was _____.

5. The surface of the moon is covered with _____.

6. In the early part of the twenty-first century, Americans expect to build a _____ on the moon.

7. The daytime temperature on the moon is _____, which is hot enough to _____.

8. There is silence on the moon because _____.

9. People's weight on the moon is _____ than their weight on Earth.

10. *Apollo 13* never made it to the moon because _____.

⭐ **ORDERING EVENTS**

Number the sentences to show the correct order. Do this without looking at the passage. Then reread the passage to check your answers.

_____ Buzz Aldrin and Neil Armstrong collected samples of rock and soil.

_____ *Apollo 13* made it safely back to earth.

_____ The *Eagle* module separated from *Apollo 11*.

_____ A plaque was placed on the moon.

_____ Neil Armstrong stepped onto the moon.

_____ Electric vehicles were used to explore the moon's surface.

⭐ MAKING INFERENCES AND CONCLUDING

Information is not always stated directly in a passage. Sometimes we make guesses—inferences or conclusions—from the information that is in the reading. The answers to these questions are not directly stated in the passage. Circle the letter of the best answer.

1. From the passage, we can conclude that
   a. people will go to the moon to lose weight.
   b. people could live comfortably on the moon if there were water there.
   c. living on the moon would be very different from life here on Earth.

2. We can infer from the passage that
   a. astronomers have always been limited by the tools they have to work with.
   b. astronomers found water on the moon 350 years ago.
   c. scientists today don't make mistakes as they did in the past.

3. The writer seems to say that
   a. humans will never get used to traveling through space.
   b. space travel will one day be an ordinary part of life.
   c. there are no longer any dangers involving space travel.

DISCUSSION

Discuss the answers to the questions with your classmates.

1. Billions of dollars have been spent on space exploration. Do you think this is a waste of taxpayer money? Why?

2. Science-fiction programs about space are very popular. Why do you think this is so? Name some of the programs currently on television that are about space travel and living.

3. The science of astronomy has existed for thousands of years. Why have people always been so curious about the stars and planets?

4. Astrology is the study of how the planets affect our lives. Do you believe in the astrological signs (signs of the Zodiac)? Why?

WRITING

Write one or more paragraphs that describe what you think life will be like on a space station.

RESEARCH AND PRESENTATION

Find out the following facts about our moon, Jupiter, Mars, and Venus.

1. Distance from Earth
2. Diameter at equator (size around the middle)
3. Size in relation to Earth
4. Average surface temperature
5. Does it have a moon or moons?
6. Who is each of these planets named after?

Now work with a partner or small group. Draw a picture of the sun, moon, Earth, and other planets that shows their distances from the sun. Then choose one of the planets, and give a short presentation about it to your class. Be prepared to answer questions.

> **DID YOU KNOW . . . ?**
> There is no "dark side" of the moon because all parts of the moon get sunlight half the time, except for a few deep craters near the poles.

The Birdman of Alcatraz

PREREADING

Answer the questions.

1. Who are some famous criminals you know about?
2. What are some famous prisons?
3. Why would a person be called "Birdman"?

The Birdman of Alcatraz

1   The story of Robert Stroud has been written many different ways. Some say he was a troubled boy from a broken home who accidentally killed someone. Others say he was a cold, **vicious** man, and a murderer who should have been **executed**. Others fall somewhere in the middle. All of them agree on one thing, though. Robert Stroud is one of the most famous American criminals of all time.

2   Robert Stroud was nineteen when he killed a man in an argument over a dance-hall girl in Juneau, Alaska. He was **sentenced to** twelve years at McNeil Island Prison in Washington State. Prison life was hard. After two years there, Stroud **stabbed** a fellow prisoner who had told the authorities Stroud was stealing food from the kitchen. Six months were added to his sentence. In 1912, he was transferred to Leavenworth Prison in Kansas.

3   Stroud had only a third-grade education. Some people thought he was stupid, including his cellmate who was taking some correspondence courses.* Stroud decided he would like to do the same. For three years he studied engineering, music, mathematics, and theology in courses from Kansas State University. He received high marks in all his studies. Stroud was now prepared for his release in the near future.

4   In March 1916, shortly before he was to be freed, Stroud killed one of the guards. He had been very angry over not being able to see his brother, who had come all the way from Alaska to visit him. He was tried, found guilty, and sentenced to hang. Stroud's mother would not accept this. She petitioned President Woodrow Wilson and his wife. She impressed them with descriptions of her son's studies, and just eight days before he was to hang, Stroud's sentence was changed to life in **solitary confinement**.

5   One day Stroud found two baby birds in the exercise yard at Leavenworth. He raised them with the help of bird books. From that point on, his interest in **ornithology** became a passion. He bought some canaries, did experiments in canary diseases, and studied and wrote about his findings. After a while, prison officials tore down the wall between Stroud's cell and another empty cell to make more room for Stroud's canaries. He obtained laboratory equipment and studied chemistry, veterinary medicine, and bacteriology.

6   By 1931, Stroud was an expert on the care and raising of canaries. He corresponded with other bird lovers all over the world. He wrote some articles that were **smuggled out** of prison and published. In 1942, he published a book called *Stroud's Digest of the Diseases of Birds*. It was considered the best work in the field. Meanwhile, Stroud's work was

---

correspondence courses: lessons received and sent by mail. Today, correspondence courses are also taken over the Internet.

making him very well known—too well known. People began to ask for Stroud's release, and this angered some prison officials.

7   In 1942, Stroud was transferred to Alcatraz. He was ordered to leave all his birds, his books, and other personal property behind. That personal property had amounted to quite a lot. It weighed 1,144 pounds and filled five containers. It included, among other things, 30 empty birdcages, 158 bottles, cans, boxes, and glass containers of chemicals, and other laboratory equipment. There were about 250 bird magazines, over 20 books on chemistry and microscopes, and many other catalogs and medical books. There were 85 pounds of various seeds, 118 feeding dishes, and 22 birds. In prison on a rocky island in San Francisco Bay, Stroud was **deprived** of all of this.

8   He then turned to the study of law and wrote an unpublished book on federal prison **reform**. He became known as the "Birdman of Alcatraz." He was the subject of newspaper and magazine articles, a book, and a movie.

9   The "Birdman" was kept in isolation for forty-two years, longer than any federal prisoner in history. In 1959, in poor health but still **seeking parole**, he was transferred to the Federal Medical Center in Springfield, Missouri, where he died four years later. He had spent fifty-six years in prison.

VOCABULARY

 MEANING

What is the meaning of the underlined words? Circle the letter of the correct answer. Use a dictionary to check your answers.

1. Robert Stroud was said to be a cold and <u>vicious</u> man.
   a. cruel with a desire to hurt
   b. insane
   c. moody

2. People said that Robert Stroud should be <u>executed</u>.
   a. put in prison
   b. killed as lawful punishment
   c. sent to another country

3. Stroud was <u>sentenced to</u> twelve years in prison.
   a. recognized
   b. given admission
   c. given a punishment of

4. Stroud <u>stabbed</u> a prisoner.
   a. poisoned
   b. strangled with his hands
   c. hit with a pointed weapon

The Birdman of Alcatraz 121

5. Stroud's sentence was changed to life in <u>solitary confinement</u>.
   a. kept in prison for the rest of his life
   b. kept completely alone in prison
   c. kept in prison and made to work

6. Stroud became interested in <u>ornithology</u>.
   a. the study of diseases
   b. the study of birds
   c. the study of animals

7. His articles on birds were <u>smuggled out</u> of prison and published.
   a. removed legally
   b. transferred
   c. taken out illegally

8. In Alcatraz, Stroud was <u>deprived</u> of all his personal property.
   a. prevented from using
   b. delayed from using
   c. thinking of using

9. Stroud began to study law and wrote a book on prison <u>reform</u>.
   a. improvements in conditions
   b. organization of prisoners
   c. violence in prison

10. In 1959, Stroud was still <u>seeking</u> <u>parole</u>.
   a. asking to be tried again
   b. asking to be forgiven for his crimes
   c. asking to be let out of prison for good behavior

 USE

Work with a partner to answer the questions. Use complete sentences.

1. What personal possession would you least want to be *deprived* of?
2. What animal is considered *vicious*?
3. What is something that is often *smuggled* out of one country and into another?
4. What is something we can learn about birds by studying *ornithology*?
5. In what area would you like to see *reform* take place?
6. What would you do with your time if you were in *solitary confinement*?
7. What is one country that does not allow criminals to be *executed*?
8. In your country, what procedure takes place before a person is *sentenced* to prison?

COMPREHENSION

SKIMMING FOR MAIN IDEAS

Quickly read to find the main idea of each paragraph, and then circle the letter of the best answer.

1. The main topic of paragraph 4 is that
   a. Stroud killed a prison guard and almost died for it.
   b. Stroud had a very bad temper.
   c. Stroud's mother came to the aid of her son by petitioning the president.

2. Paragraph 5 is mainly about
   a. how Stroud found two baby birds.
   b. the beginning of Stroud's interest in birds.
   c. Stroud's kindness to animals.

3. The main topic of paragraph 6 is that
   a. Stroud became an expert on bird diseases.
   b. Stroud became known for his canaries.
   c. Stroud wanted to be released.

4. Paragraph 7 is mainly about the fact that
   a. Stroud had to leave his birds behind.
   b. Stroud was sent to Alcatraz unfairly.
   c. Stroud was transferred to Alcatraz without his belongings.

SCANNING FOR DETAILS

Reread the passage quickly to find key words and phrases from the questions. Then write the correct answer on the line.

1. While Robert Stroud was in prison, he took courses from
   _____ University.

2. After Robert Stroud killed a man in Juneau, Alaska, he was sentenced to
   _____ years in _____ Prison.

3. While in prison, Robert Stroud cared for and studied _____.

4. While in prison, Robert Stroud studied _____,
   _____, _____, and theology.

5. Before he went to prison, Stroud had only a _____ education.

6. When Stroud was transferred to Alcatraz, he had to leave behind

   _____.

7. After Stroud killed a guard and was sentenced to hang, his

   _____ asked President _____ to let him live.

8. Alcatraz Prison was located _____.

9. Instead of being hanged for his crime, Robert Stroud was given a

   sentence of _____.

10. In 1942, Stroud published a book on _____ that

    was considered the best work in the field.

 ## ORDERING EVENTS

**Number the sentences to show the correct order. Do this without looking
at the passage. Then reread the passage to check your answers.**

_____ Stroud started taking correspondence courses.

_____ Stroud was sent to a prison in Washington state.

_____ Stroud was transferred to Alcatraz.

_____ Stroud killed a man in a dispute over a dance-hall girl.

_____ Stroud became interested in ornithology.

_____ Stroud became famous as the "Birdman of Alcatraz."

_____ Stroud's mother asked Woodrow Wilson to save her son's life.

MAKING INFERENCES AND CONCLUDING

**Information is not always stated directly in a passage. Sometimes we
make guesses—inferences or conclusions—from the information that is
in the reading. The answers to these questions are not directly stated in
the passage. Circle the letter of the best answer.**

1. From the passage, we can conclude that

   a. some people believed that Stroud should be set free.

   b. Stroud became famous because of the crimes he committed.

   c. President Wilson showed no pity toward Stroud and his mother.

2. We can infer from the passage that

   a. from the time of his first imprisonment, Stroud never had another
      chance to be free.

   b. Stroud was well treated by prison officials at Leavenworth.

   c. Stroud probably didn't mind being transferred to Alcatraz.

 **124** UNIT 17

3. The writer seems to say that

   a. in spite of his lack of childhood education, Stroud proved to be highly intelligent.

   b. Stroud got along better with people than with animals.

   c. Stroud's transfer to Alcatraz made him completely lose interest in life.

DISCUSSION

Discuss the answers to the questions with your classmates.

1. Do you think prisoners should study and get degrees in prison? Why?
2. How are crimes punished differently in different countries?
3. Do you think laws are too easy on criminals today? Why?
4. Do you think the "Birdman" was treated fairly? Why?

WRITING

Write one or more paragraphs that discuss at least two reasons for and two reasons against capital punishment (execution for a crime).

RESEARCH AND PRESENTATION

Below is a list of famous criminals. Find out what crime(s) each committed and how he or she died.

1. William H. Bonney ("Billy the Kid")
2. Ma Barker
3. Al "Scarface" Capone
4. John Dillinger
5. Jesse James
6. Albert di Salvo

Now work with a partner or small group. Prepare a short presentation about one of these criminals. What crimes did he or she commit? How was he or she caught and punished? Was this punishment fair? How would a criminal like this be punished today?

DID YOU KNOW . . . ?

Alcatraz is considered one of America's most haunted places. Over the years, tour guides, park rangers, security guards, and night watchmen have reported hearing screams, moans, cries, footsteps, and other noises, and quite a few say they have seen the ghosts of prisoners and even soldiers who once lived on the island.

A History of Animation

PREREADING

Answer the questions.

1. Do you like animated films? Why?
2. Who is the most famous animator you know?
3. Who are some famous animated characters? Which is your favorite?

A History of Animation

1   Six-year-old Andy is in his room playing with his toys. His favorite is a cowboy doll named Woody. When Andy leaves his room, all the toys **come to life**. Woody tells them it is Andy's birthday. The toys begin to worry that Andy will get a new toy that he'll like better than them. At his party, Andy opens his last present—an action figure named Buzz Lightyear. Buzz wears a spacesuit. He doesn't know he's a toy. He believes he's **on a mission** to save the planet. All the other toys love Buzz Lightyear—all except Woody. Woody is upset. He throws Buzz out the window!

2   *Toy Story* was a movie made by Walt Disney Productions and Pixar Animation Studios. It was shown for the first time in 1995 and was the first full-length computer-generated movie. That means it was the first movie ever made entirely on computers. It was a big success, and it opened the way for more computer-generated films, such as *A Bug's Life*, *Toy Story 2*, *Finding Nemo*, *Cars*, and many others.

3   Animation is the process of making a drawing appear to move, and it **has been around** for centuries. In earlier times it was done with simple but clever devices that made pieces of paper move quickly. To the human eye, the **figures** in the pictures appeared to move. It took hundreds of drawings for just a few moments of action. Even in more modern times, animation was a long and difficult process. Artists spent hundreds of hours making drawings. Each drawing showed a figure with a slight change. Thousands of these drawings were put together and photographed on a length of film called a reel. When the film was played back rapidly, it made an animated cartoon.

4   The first animations on celluloid, or clear sheets of film, were made around 1914 by Earl Hurd. Hurd learned that by using celluloid, one **image** could be put on top of another. For example, an artist could draw a cat. If only the cat's ears were going to move, the cat didn't have to be drawn over and over. Only the ears had to be drawn and placed over the rest of the cat. Animated cartoons such as *Felix the Cat*, *Koko the Clown*, and, of course, *Mickey Mouse* became very popular.

5   Walt Disney made great changes in animation. He was the first to add color and sound to a cartoon film. In 1937, he produced the first full-length animated movie, *Snow White and the Seven Dwarfs*. In those days, making an animated movie was a slow and difficult process. For *Snow White* alone, Disney used 300 artists. They worked as teams 24 hours a day, seven days a week for over six months. The cost to make the film was six times what Walt Disney thought it would be, but the movie was a huge success. Afterward, Disney made one animated **hit** movie after another. Eventually there were studios all over the world making animated films.

6   Today, the large animation studios are using computers to make most of their films. Computer animation uses very advanced technology. The history of computer animation started almost fifty years ago, and developing computer animation was a slow process that took many years. First, a computer-drawing system was created by General Motors and IBM to help design cars. Then in 1961, Ivan Sutherland, a student at MIT (Massachusetts Institute of Technology), designed a computer program called Sketchpad. This program allowed a person to draw a figure on an electronic drawing **pad** with a special pen called a light pen. The pad sent signals that made lines and marks appear on a computer screen.

In the 1960s and 1970s, computer animation was used mostly for industrial and scientific purposes. For example, it was used in weather maps to **track** storms and other weather events. But in the late 1970s and early 1980s, George Lucas and Steven Spielberg began using computers to create exciting sounds and images—special effects—in their films.

7   In 1986, a group of animators—people who create animation—got together and created their own company called Pixar. It took them twenty years of dreaming, planning, and hard work to create *Toy Story*. First, they had to come up with the idea for the story and write it down. Then they drew the characters. Each character was drawn several times before the final character was decided upon. Sculptures of each of the characters were made. Then the actors, such as Tom Hanks and Tim Allen, recorded their voices. The artists watched the actors carefully. Their expressions gave them ideas for the looks and movements of the cartoon characters. Finally the animators were ready to create the images on their computers. They created a new computer program called RenderMan. It became Pixar's greatest **contribution** to the world of computer animation.

8   Today computer animation is used in movies, television, music videos, commercials, video games, and in science and business all over the world. Even ordinary people can create simple animated figures on their home computers. Technology continues to improve, making animation faster, easier, and more realistic. Maybe someday computer images will be so advanced that we won't be able to tell the difference between real people and animated figures!

9   And what happened to Woody and Buzz Lightyear? They eventually **got trapped** together in a dangerous situation and learned to work together.

VOCABULARY

⭐ MEANING

Complete each definition with one of the following. Guess your answers, and then check them with a dictionary.

come to life	has been around	image	pad	contribution
on a mission	figures	hit	track	got trapped

1. People who are _____ are performing a work or deed that they believe they have a special duty to do.

2. If something _____ for a while, it has existed somewhere for a length of time.

3. _____ are the shapes of human or animal bodies in art.

4. You _____ if you couldn't get out of the place you were in because something was keeping you there.

5. Things _____ when they suddenly have movement and speech.

6. A _____ is something smooth and hard that a person can write or draw on.

7. Something that helps others is a _____.

8. Something is a _____ if it is very successful.

9. To _____ is to follow the path of something that is moving.

10. A picture of a person, animal, or scene is an _____.

⭐ USE

Work with a partner to answer the questions. Use complete sentences.

1. What movie was recently a big *hit*?
2. What is an invention that *has been around* for a relatively short time?
3. What is your favorite photographic *image*?
4. Why do scientists *track* storms?
5. What does a writing *pad* look like?
6. What are some cartoon characters that are *on a mission* to save the world?
7. What would you do if you *got trapped* in a burning building?
8. Who is a person who has made a great *contribution* to the world?

A History of Animation **129**

COMPREHENSION

SKIMMING FOR MAIN IDEAS

Quickly read to find the main idea of each paragraph, and then circle the letter of the best answer.

1. Paragraph 3 is mainly about
   a. the devices that early animators used.
   b. the way animation was done in the past.
   c. the use of reels to create animated cartoons.

2. The main topic of paragraph 5 is
   a. the changes Walt Disney made in animation.
   b. the cost and effort it took for Disney to make *Snow White and the Seven Dwarfs*.
   c. the popularity of Disney's animated films.

3. The main topic of paragraph 6 is
   a. the development of the computer program called Sketchpad.
   b. the technology that is used in computer animation.
   c. the first attempts at computer animation.

4. Paragraph 7 is mainly about
   a. the process Pixar used to create *Toy Story*.
   b. Pixar's greatest contribution to computer animation.
   c. the creation of the company called Pixar.

SCANNING FOR DETAILS

Reread the passage quickly to find key words and phrases from the questions. Each sentence has an incorrect fact. Cross out the incorrect fact, and write the correct answer above it.

1. *Toy Story* was the first full-length animated movie.

2. The first animated cartoons were made by putting the photographs of thousands of drawings on a board.

3. Each drawing on a reel showed a different figure.

4. Celluloid was made of long lengths of film.

5. The advantage of using celluloid was that artists didn't have to draw the same image twice.

6. Earl Hurd was the first to make a cartoon film with color and sound.

7. Sketchpad was a computer program that allowed people to draw figures on a computer screen with a special pen called a light pen.

8. Lucas and Spielberg used computers to create animated figures in their films in the late 1970s and early 1980s.

9. During the creation of *Toy Story*, the artists watched the actors carefully in order to get ideas for the voices of the cartoon characters.

10. Pixar's greatest contribution to the world of movies is a program called RenderMan.

⭐ ORDERING EVENTS

Number the sentences to show the correct order. Do this without looking at the passage. Then reread the passage to check your answers.

_____ Ivan Sutherland developed the Sketchpad program.

_____ *Toy Story* was made by Disney and Pixar.

_____ Animated cartoons were made on film reels.

_____ Walt Disney made the first full-length animated movie.

_____ Lucas and Spielberg began using computerized images in their films.

_____ Simple devices made figures appear to move by making drawings on paper move quickly in front of the eye.

_____ Earl Hurd made the first animations on celluloid.

_____ Animated cartoons like *Felix the Cat* became popular.

Information is not always stated directly in a passage. Sometimes we make guesses—inferences or conclusions—from the information that is in the reading. The answers to these questions are not directly stated in the passage. Circle the letter of the best answer.

1. From the passage, we can conclude that
   a. celluloid was not a big improvement on the slow, difficult process of animation.
   b. people liked animated cartoons on reels better than celluloid cartoons.
   c. computer animation was not originally developed for use by the film industry.

2. We can infer from the passage that
   a. Disney was discouraged by the difficulty of making the first full-length animated film.
   b. Disney influenced other studios to make animated movies.
   c. Soon after Disney made *Snow White*, the process of animation became faster and easier.

3. The writer seems to say that
   a. animated figures will eventually take the place of people in movies.
   b. the uses of animation are not limited to movies.
   c. there isn't much more that can be done with animation in the future.

DISCUSSION

Discuss the answers to the questions with your classmates.

1. What is your favorite animated movie?
2. Why do people of all ages like animation?
3. Do you think movies use too many special effects? Why?
4. What are some uses of animation outside of movies?

WRITING

What if animation were so advanced that you couldn't tell the difference between an animated figure and a human figure? Write one or more paragraphs about the advantages and disadvantages of animated figures that look like real people.

RESEARCH AND PRESENTATION

Below is a list of animated films. Find out when and in what country each film was made.

1. *The Adventures of Juku the Dog*
2. *Camel's Dance*
3. *Castle in the Sky*
4. *Creature Comforts*
5. *The Magic Lake*
6. *Mulan*
7. *Pinocchio*
8. *When the Wind Blows*

Now work with a partner or small group. Choose an animated film, and create a short presentation about it for your class. Include a summary of the story and description and/or drawings of one or more of the characters. Say when and where the film was made. Be prepared to answer questions.

DID YOU KNOW . . . ?

The first examples of animation can be found in Stone Age cave paintings, where animals are drawn with multiple legs on top of each other, showing a sense of motion.

The Google Guys

PREREADING

Answer the questions.

1. How often do you use a computer to find information?
2. Do you use the Google search engine? Why?
3. Is the invention of the Google search engine important? Why?

The Google Guys

1   In 1996, two **graduate students** at Stanford University had a grand dream. Larry Page and Sergey Brin wanted to make information available to everybody, so they started a research project. Two years later, they started a company in a friend's garage. Today they are billionaires, and that company is Google.

2   Google is a search engine—a way of searching for information on the Internet. In 1996, there were a few search engines. Page and Brin believed they had a better **technique** to search the web, so they created Google. Google comes from the word *googol*, which is a 1 with 100 zeros after it. Everybody loved Google because it was fast and easy to use. More and more people began to use it, and the company grew quickly. Eventually, so many people used Google that in 2006 the verb "google" was added to the dictionary. Today, 70 to 80 percent of computer users use Google, and the Google search engine receives about a billion search requests a day.

3   Sergey Brin was born in Moscow, Russia, in August 1973. His family immigrated to the United States when he was six and settled in Maryland. Brin was interested in computers and math when he was very young, and his parents encouraged him. His father was a mathematics professor, and his mother worked for NASA (the National Aeronautics and Space Administration). In school, Brin was a star in the chess club and math team, but he also loved to have fun and play jokes on people. He received a Bachelor's degree in mathematics and computer science from the University of Maryland. He then went to Stanford and earned his Master's degree. From there, he entered Stanford's Ph.D. program. The rest is history.

4   Larry Page was born in Lansing, Michigan, in March 1973. His parents were both computer scientists. As a boy, Page **idolized** Nikola Tesla, the inventor of the ac (alternating current) system of electricity. He says he fell in love with computers at age six. He was a brilliant boy and was often smarter than even his best teachers. Everyone knew he would do something great one day. Page got a Bachelor's degree in computer engineering from the University of Michigan. He earned a Master's from Stanford before entering their Ph.D. program. When Page and Brin met, they didn't like each other very much, but soon they realized that they had an interest in common—making a better search engine.

5   Google's headquarters are in Mountain View, California. There are several buildings called "the Googleplex." Page and Brin didn't want their company to be like other big corporations. Their **motto** was "Do no evil." They didn't want the company to hurt people or the planet in any way. For example, the company uses solar energy—power from the sun—for its electricity. The main **lobby** of the headquarters is decorated with a piano

and colorful lamps from the 1960s. The hallways are full of toys and sports equipment, such as exercise balls and bicycles. All the employees can use the company **recreational facilities**. There are exercise rooms, video games, and a roller rink. There's a pool table, Foosball, Ping-Pong, and even a baby grand piano! There are also free snacks and cereals, juices, sodas, and coffee.

6   Page and Brin never believed in a strict and formal atmosphere. If you visited Googleplex, you would see employees playing games and having fun. Of course, they also do work! But all Google engineers are encouraged to spend one day a week on any project that interests them. This has actually **worked out** very well for the company. Engineers created several new Google services during these times off.

7   Google also has a tradition of playing April Fool's jokes.* In 2002, they claimed that pigeons** were the secret behind their successful search engine. In 2004, they put up Google Lunar, which advertised jobs on the moon. In 2005, they advertised a new drink called Google Gulp that was supposed to improve the brain. Every year there is a clever new joke. One year, around the first of April, they brought out a new e-mail service called Gmail. Everyone thought it was a joke!

8   The success of Google and its founders is no joke, however. Google continues to grow and has bought several smaller companies. It continues to improve on products and services, and it goes on creating new ones, such as Google News, Google Earth, Google Maps, Google Video, and many more. Page and Brin, the "**wonder** boys," are now among the richest men in the world. Nevertheless, you can still catch Page going to work on his in-line skates or **snapping together** a robot with his Lego bricks. You can still see Brin with a **mischievous** look in his eye, thinking up a clever new trick.

---

* *April Fool's jokes*: People in some countries celebrate April 1st by playing jokes or tricks on each other. Then they say, "April Fool!"
** *pigeons*: birds with round bodies and small heads, usually a gray or white color

VOCABULARY

⭐ MEANING

What is the meaning of the underlined words? Circle the letter of the correct answer. Use a dictionary to check your answers.

1. Page and Brin were <u>graduate students</u> at Stanford University.
   a. people preparing to graduate for the first time
   b. people doing studies after receiving their first degree
   c. people studying for two degrees at once

2. Page and Brin had a better <u>technique</u> for searching the web.
   a. way of doing something
   b. talent or ability for doing something
   c. knowledge of something

3. Page <u>idolized</u> Nikola Tesla.
   a. knew very well
   b. thought of very highly
   c. acted very much like

4. The Google company <u>motto</u> is "Do no evil."
   a. a few words that guide people's actions
   b. a sentence that explains what a company does or sells
   c. a rule that everyone must obey

5. The main <u>lobby</u> is decorated with colorful lamps.
   a. a large room where people have parties and formal dinners
   b. a place where businesspeople meet and make important decisions
   c. an area at the entrance of a building that goes to rooms inside a building

6. There are <u>recreational facilities</u> for the employees.
   a. quiet places where people can do their work
   b. places where people can sit and eat or drink
   c. places where people can play games or do sports

7. This <u>worked out</u> for the company.
   a. caused problems
   b. had a good result
   c. made things different

8. Page and Brin are called the "<u>wonder</u> boys."
   a. unusually good or excellent
   b. particularly fast or strong
   c. extremely beautiful or exciting

9. Page was <u>snapping together</u> a robot.
   a. putting one part into another
   b. making a design for
   c. laying one thing on top of another

10. Brin has a <u>mischievous</u> look.
    a. highly intelligent
    b. very serious
    c. playfully bad

 USE

Work with a partner to answer the questions. Use complete sentences.

1. What are some things that can be found at *recreational facilities*?
2. Why does a club or organization have a *motto*?
3. Who is someone you *idolized* as child?
4. What is one *technique* that you have that is particularly good?
5. What is something that can be made by *snapping together* its pieces?
6. What is something that has *worked out* well for you recently?
7. What purpose does a *lobby* serve in a business or hotel?
8. What are some *mischievous* things that children do?

COMPREHENSION

 SKIMMING FOR MAIN IDEAS

Quickly read to find the main idea of each paragraph, and then circle the letter of the best answer.

1. Paragraph 2 is mainly about
   a. why Page and Brin created Google.
   b. why people like to use Google.
   c. how Google grew very fast.

2. The main topic of paragraph 5 is
   a. how Page and Brin want to do what is good for the environment.
   b. the type of company that Page and Brin have created.
   c. what the workers do at the Google headquarters.

3. The main topic of paragraph 6 is
   a. how Google employees like to have fun.
   b. how an unusual company policy works.
   c. why Page and Brin believe in an informal atmosphere.

4. The last paragraph is mainly about
    a. the ongoing success of Google.
    b. the personalities of Page and Brin.
    c. how Page and Brin became rich men.

⭐ SCANNING FOR DETAILS

Reread the passage quickly to find key words and phrases from the questions. Circle *T* if the sentence is true. Circle *F* if the sentence is false.

1.	Page and Brin started Google in 1996.	T	F
2.	The word *googol* means "search."	T	F
3.	A search engine finds information on the web.	T	F
4.	Brin's parents wanted him to learn about computers.	T	F
5.	Brin earned his Bachelor's degree at the University of Maryland and his Master's at Stanford.	T	F
6.	Page wasn't interested in computers until he went to college.	T	F
7.	Page and Brin liked each other the first day they met.	T	F
8.	Google employees have games to play with and rooms to exercise in.	T	F
9.	Google employees are encouraged to use two days a week for their own projects.	T	F
10.	Gmail wasn't an April Fool's Day joke.	T	F

⭐ ORDERING EVENTS

Number the sentences to show the correct order. Do this without looking at the passage. Then reread the passage to check your answers.

_____ The headquarters of Google was built in Mountain View.

_____ Page and Brin entered the Ph.D. program at Stanford.

_____ Page and Brin started a company in a friend's garage.

_____ Sergey Brin and his family immigrated to America.

_____ Google introduced new services such as Google News and Google Earth.

_____ Page and Brin began a research project to create a better search engine.

_____ Larry Page got a Bachelor's degree from the University of Michigan.

⭐ MAKING INFERENCES AND CONCLUDING

Information is not always stated directly in a passage. Sometimes we make guesses—inferences or conclusions—from the information that is in the reading. The answers to these questions are not directly stated in the passage. Circle the letter of the best answer.

1. From the passage, we can conclude that
   a. Page's and Brin's childhood interests contributed to their future achievements.
   b. Neither Page's nor Brin's parents were happy about their interest in computers as children.
   c. Most people who knew Page and Brin were surprised that they became so successful.

2. The writer seems to say that
   a. if Page and Brin had been more traditional businessmen, they would have been even more successful.
   b. Page and Brin cared more about the success of their company than about their employees.
   c. Page's and Brin's unusual way of doing business helped to make Google a big success.

3. We can infer from the passage that
   a. success has changed the personalities of Page and Brin.
   b. Page and Brin aren't interested in making Google grow into a larger company.
   c. Page and Brin try not to be personally affected by Google's growth and success.

DISCUSSION

Discuss the answers to the questions with your classmates.

1. In what ways does success change people?
2. Do you think it is possible not to be changed by great success? Why?
3. If you suddenly became a great success, how do you think it would change you and your life?
4. Would you like to own your own company? Why?

WRITING

Imagine that you could own your own company. Write one or more paragraphs about the company. Be sure to give the company a name, describe what products or services the company would provide, and how you would run it.

RESEARCH AND PRESENTATION

Find out what products or services the following companies provide and where their headquarters are located.

1. AT&T
2. Avon
3. DuPont
4. Hilton
5. Kia
6. Nike
7. Sony
8. Virgin

Now work with a partner or small group. Create a print, TV, or radio ad for one of the products. Present it to your class, and be prepared to answer questions.

DID YOU KNOW...?

The SAGE computer system of the 1950s was the largest, heaviest, and most expensive computer system ever built. It weighed 250 tons, had 60,000 vacuum tubes, and required over 20,000 square feet.

All-American Football

PREREADING

Answer the questions.

1. What is the most popular sport in your country?
2. What do you know about American football?
3. Do you like football? Why?

All-American Football

1   Football is not just a game in America. It's an event—a *big* event. Millions of people attend football games or watch them on television. Thousands of others play football themselves on professional, school, or neighborhood teams, or just with friends. The games are often only a part of the colorful spectacles that go with them. Parades and marching bands, cheerleaders, and cheering fans with **banners** and horns are all part of the festivities surrounding football.

2   Football has its beginnings in soccer and rugby. All have the same objective, which is to get the ball to the **opponent's** goal and score points. Soccer was played in England in the eleventh century. The ball was advanced only by kicking it. In 1839, rugby was born when a frustrated English soccer player picked up the ball and ran down the field with it. American college students played soccer in the 1800s, but the game was called "football." Then, in 1874, a new form of the football game developed that combined both soccer and rugby. Players not only kicked the ball but also advanced it by running with it and passing it to teammates.

3   American football developed into a rough **contact sport**. Because protective equipment was not used in those days, it was quite dangerous. In 1905, 18 players were killed, and 159 seriously injured. President Theodore Roosevelt threatened **to ban** football if the roughness didn't stop. The rules committee began changing the rules, and eventually football developed into the game it is today.

     The basic idea of football is very simple. The team that has the ball runs with it or throws or kicks it toward the other team's goal while the other team tries to stop them. Each time a team reaches the other's goal, it scores a certain number of points. They want to get the ball so they can score. The team that scores the most points wins the game.

4   The teams play for one hour, divided into four quarters. There is always a halftime break of at least fifteen minutes. The teams are allowed timeouts, which are times when the clock is stopped and the team can get together to talk about **strategy**. The clock is also stopped when players are injured and when there are penalties given for playing against the rules. Sometimes new players are **substituted for** those who have already played. There are also breaks for television commercials. With all this going on, the one-hour game can easily take up to two and a half or three hours!

5   Football in the United States is played by more than 600 colleges and universities. The stadiums in which they play are often called "bowls." At the end of the college season, usually in December or January, the best college teams are invited to play against each other in "bowl games."

There is the Orange Bowl in Miami, the Sugar Bowl in New Orleans, the Cotton Bowl in Dallas, and the Gator Bowl in Jacksonville, Florida. These games attract large crowds and offer colorful marching bands and **squads** of cheerleaders who perform a combination of gymnastics, dancing, and **drills** to entertain the audience and encourage the players.

6   The greatest of all the bowl games is the Rose Bowl held in Pasadena, California, since 1902. It attracts a crowd of over 100,000 people every year and is played on New Year's Day. The game itself, however, is not the main attraction. What thousands of people come to see and millions more watch on their televisions internationally is the Tournament of Roses Parade. It is a breathtaking parade of **floats** covered entirely with flowers, petals, seeds, and other flower parts. Marching bands and floats from around the world participate and compete for prizes for the best and most beautiful float. There are circus scenes and tropical forests and giant spaceships, all covered with flowers. The parade is a spectacle of beauty that is unequaled anywhere.

7   After the Rose Bowl and the end of the college football season, fans turn their attention to the professional teams who are playing their own championship games. The final play-off game to decide the season's champion team is called the Super Bowl. Once again, the game is less important than all the activity surrounding it. It has now become a tradition to have "Super Bowl" parties on "Super Bowl Sunday." Usually, friends gather at one household. Everyone brings food, and some partygoers bring extra televisions that are placed outdoors and in rooms throughout the house. That way the guests, in between eating and talking, can watch the game from wherever they are.

8   Even those not interested in football look forward to seeing the halftime show. This has become quite an **extravaganza**. In recent years, top entertainers have performed at the Super Bowl. Light shows and fireworks displays, marching bands, cheerleaders, and dancers are all part of halftime. It is watched by millions of viewers around the country. Part sport, part entertainment, football has become an important part of the American way of life.

VOCABULARY

⭐ MEANING

Complete each definition with one of the following. Guess your answers, and then check them with a dictionary.

banners	contact sport	strategy	squads	floats
opponent's	to ban	substituted for	drills	extravaganza

1. A sport in which the players touch each other is a _____.
2. An _____ is an elaborate, spectacular form of entertainment.
3. _____ is to forbid something, usually by law.
4. The person on the opposite side's team is on the _____ team.
5. When something or someone is put in place of another, it is

   _____.

6. Groups of people working in teams are _____.
7. _____ are large, flat vehicles showing special scenes or shows

   and that are drawn in a procession.
8. Long pieces of cloth on which words or signs are painted are

   _____.

9. _____ are exercises that a team has been trained to do

   together.
10. _____ is skillful planning.

⭐ USE

Work with a partner to answer the questions. Use complete sentences.

1. What event has become an *extravaganza* in your country?
2. In what area besides sports are people required to do *drills*?
3. What team is a strong *opponent* of one of your country's sports teams?
4. At what events are *banners* displayed in your country?
5. What ingredient is often *substituted for* another in food and soft drinks?
6. What is an area other than sports in which *strategy* is important?
7. What activity has the government of your country threatened *to ban* in

   the past or present?
8. What is a *contact sport* other than football?

COMPREHENSION

SKIMMING FOR MAIN IDEAS

Quickly read to find the main idea of each paragraph, and then circle the letter of the best answer.

1. Paragraph 2 is mainly about
   a. how football originated from soccer and rugby.
   b. how soccer was played by American college students.
   c. how football is similar to rugby.

2. The main topic in paragraph 3 is that
   a. American football did not have special equipment.
   b. American football was a rough sport.
   c. President Theodore Roosevelt did not like football.

3. Paragraph 5 is mainly about
   a. the entertainment provided at the stadiums.
   b. the large crowds at the bowls.
   c. football games played by colleges and universities.

4. The main topic of the last paragraph is that
   a. top entertainers want to perform at the Super Bowl.
   b. football games are watched only by sports fans.
   c. football today has become a popular form of entertainment.

SCANNING FOR DETAILS

Reread the passage quickly to find key words and phrases from the questions. Then circle the letter of the correct answer.

1. In football, the team with the ball tries to get it
   a. in a basket.
   b. over their goal.
   c. to the other team's goal.

2. President Theodore Roosevelt threatened to stop football because it was getting too
   a. popular.
   b. dangerous.
   c. noisy.

3. Football originated with
   a. basketball.
   b. soccer.
   c. baseball.

4. A football game is divided into
   a. two halves.
   b. three thirds.
   c. four quarters.

5. The stadiums in which football games are held are often called
   a. bowls.
   b. rinks.
   c. coliseums.

6. Along with football games, there are often
   a. circuses.
   b. races.
   c. marching bands.

7. The final play-off game for professional teams is the
   a. Gator Bowl.
   b. Super Bowl.
   c. Rose Bowl.

8. Rugby was started in England in
   a. 1839.
   b. 1874.
   c. 1905.

9. The Rose Bowl is played on
   a. the first day of the season.
   b. a Sunday.
   c. New Year's Day.

10. During timeouts
    a. the team discusses strategy.
    b. the cheerleaders perform.
    c. the rules are sometimes changed.

 ORDERING EVENTS

Number the sentences to show the correct order. Do this without looking at the passage. Then reread the passage to check your answers.

_____ Rugby was born when an English soccer player ran with the ball.

_____ Football developed into a rough sport.

_____ The Super Bowl became a popular American event.

_____ Eighteen football players were killed and 159 seriously wounded in a single year.

_____ New rules were applied to the game of football.

_____ A new form of game developed in America that combined soccer and rugby.

_____ Soccer was played in England in the eleventh century.

_____ The first Rose Bowl game was played in Pasadena.

⭐ MAKING INFERENCES AND CONCLUDING

Information is not always stated directly in a passage. Sometimes we make guesses—inferences or conclusions—from the information that is in the reading. The answers to these questions are not directly stated in the passage. Circle the letter of the best answer.

1. From the passage, we can conclude that
   a. football will eventually lose its popularity in America.
   b. modern football is as much a form of entertainment as it is a sports event.
   c. football is more popular as a college sport than as a professional sport.

2. We can infer from the passage that
   a. the use of protective equipment makes the modern game of football more interesting to watch.
   b. the game of modern football is not much different from the rugby played by American college students many years ago.
   c. soccer, football, and rugby have several common elements.

3. The writer seems to say that
   a. football often brings Americans together in social situations.
   b. if it weren't for professional teams, football wouldn't be popular in America.
   c. football games are usually watched by people who are athletes themselves.

DISCUSSION

Discuss the answers to the questions with your classmates.

1. What customs are associated with sports in your country?
2. Do you think professional athletes should be paid such high salaries?
3. Who is your favorite sports star? Why?
4. Do you think professional players should be allowed to participate in the Olympics? Why?

WRITING

Why are sports so popular? Write one or more paragraphs that give two examples of popular sports and reasons why people like them.

RESEARCH AND PRESENTATION

For the sports of ice hockey, baseball, cricket, basketball, and soccer, find out the following facts.

1. The number of players on a team
2. The uniforms that are worn
3. The kind of equipment that is used
4. How the game is scored

Now work with a partner or small group. Choose one sport, and prepare a short presentation about it. Include information about all of the facts you researched and one person who is a famous player of the sport. Be prepared to answer questions.

DID YOU KNOW . . . ?
Americans eat almost 30 million pounds of snack foods on Super Bowl Sunday, including 11 million pounds of potato chips, 8.2 million pounds of tortilla chips, 4.3 million pounds of pretzels, 3.8 million pounds of popcorn, and 2.5 million pounds of snack nuts!

The History of Rock

PREREADING

Answer the questions.

1. What rock music singers or groups do you know about?
2. Is rock music popular in your country? Why?
3. Do you like rock music? Why?

The History of Rock

1   In 1955, rock and roll was born in America. That year Bill Haley and His Comets performed "Rock Around the Clock," the first big hit of this new style of music. It was first known as "rock and roll" and then simply as "rock." It would become the most popular type of American music from that point on, and it would always appeal to young people as an expression of their search for identity and independence.

2   Rock and roll of the mid-1950s grew mainly out of rhythm and blues. It was a dance music of African-Americans that combined blues, jazz, and gospel styles. Rock was also influenced by country and western music. At this time, rock and roll performers such as Chuck Berry and Little Richard were very popular. However, the most successful early rock and roll performer was Elvis Presley. He **reigned** as the "king" of rock and roll for a long time.

3   Just as rock and roll **originated** from a combination of music styles, it developed into many different forms. During the 1960s rock music was made up of a number of different styles. It ranged from the surf music of the Beach Boys and the hard rock of the Rolling Stones to the heavy metal music of Deep Purple and Jimi Hendrix. One of the big differences between 1960s rock and earlier rock and roll was the use of electronic instruments and sound equipment. It was also freer and more **experimental**.

4   British groups played an important part in the development of rock music in the 1960s. The Beatles were the first British group to **achieve** success in the United States. Their first hit recordings were "I Want to Hold Your Hand," "Can't Buy Me Love," and "Love Me Do." Other successful rock and roll groups originated in Britain, such as the Rolling Stones, The Who, Pink Floyd, and the Animals. Meanwhile in America, San Francisco was becoming the leading center of rock with such groups as Jefferson Airplane and the Grateful Dead.

5   In the 1970s, rock was as popular as ever, but many of the rock groups of the 1960s broke up. Others like the Rolling Stones and Grateful Dead continued to perform and record. The 1970s and early 1980s were years of great technological progress in the production of rock music. **Sophisticated** instruments and recording equipment were used, including tape recorders with several tracks, and **synthesizers**. Synthesizers are electronic musical instruments. They are often called keyboards. Unlike traditional instruments, synthesizers use electronic signals. They make the sounds of traditional instruments, like a piano, guitar, or organ, but they can also create new sounds that have never been heard before. All the sounds can be put together and played at once. Like the 1960s, the 1970s also saw the development of different styles. Heavy metal used extreme **amplification** and long electric guitar **solos**. Some of the best-known heavy-metal rock performers included Alice Cooper, Grand Funk Railroad, and Aerosmith.

6   The rock music of the late 1970s once again **emphasized** the rhythm and energy of early rock and roll. It also helped produce the styles of the 1980s and 1990s. Today, rock is still played by bands throughout the United States and the rest of the world. Original rock groups and new bands play to huge audiences who never seem to tire of the rock beat. Rock is still wide open to **diversity**, experimentation, and invention. It is still the music of young people, but today, older people who listened to rock when they were young also continue to enjoy it. In many ways rock is a mirror of American culture. It is energetic and unpredictable. It is a mixture of styles that work together, and it offers something to people of all ages. It seems Americans will always be rockin' round the clock.

VOCABULARY

 MEANING

What is the meaning of the underlined words? Circle the letter of the correct answer. Use a dictionary to check your answers.

1. Elvis Presley <u>reigned</u> as the "king" of rock and roll for a decade.
   a. won
   b. performed
   c. ruled

2. Rock and roll <u>originated</u> from a combination of music styles.
   a. was introduced
   b. was created
   c. copied

3. Rock music of the 1960s was more <u>experimental</u> than earlier rock and roll.
   a. things were done the same way as in the past
   b. one method only was used
   c. new ways of making music were tried

4. The Beatles were the first British group to <u>achieve</u> success in the United States.
   a. gain
   b. miss
   c. begin

5. More <u>sophisticated</u> instruments were used in the 1970s.
   a. refined
   b. simple
   c. different

6. <u>Synthesizers</u> were also used in the 1970s.
   a. electric guitars and loudspeakers
   b. electronic instruments with a single sound
   c. electronic keyboards that make many different sounds

7. The heavy-metal style of music used extreme <u>amplification</u>.
   a. quiet rhythm
   b. increased volume
   c. fast beat

8. The heavy-metal music also made use of long electric guitar <u>solos</u>.
   a. many things combined
   b. several different sounds
   c. performances by one member of the group

9. The rock music of the late 1970s <u>emphasized</u> the rhythm of early rock and roll.
   a. gave importance to
   b. forgot
   c. included

10. Rock music today is still open to <u>diversity</u>.
    a. unity
    b. difficulties
    c. differences

 USE

Work with a partner to answer the questions. Use complete sentences.

1. Who is someone known to *achieve* great success in music in your country?
2. What are some examples of the *diversity* of music today?
3. What can *synthesizers* do that single instruments cannot do?
4. What is an area besides music in which things are very *experimental* today?
5. What type of *solos* do you like: vocal, drum, or instrumental?
6. What type of traditional music in your country *emphasized* the rhythms or ways of life in the past?
7. Who is a musician who has *reigned* in the music world in the past three decades?
8. What is a characteristic of *sophisticated* people?

COMPREHENSION

 SKIMMING FOR THE MAIN IDEAS

Quickly read to find the main idea of each paragraph, and then circle the letter of the best answer.

1. Paragraph 1 is mainly about
   a. what rock music means to young people.
   b. the first appearance of rock and roll in America.
   c. the change from "rock and roll" to simply "rock."

2. The main topic of paragraph 2 is
    a. the life of Elvis Presley as the "king" of rock and roll.
    b. the origin of rock and roll music.
    c. the difference between rock and roll and African dance music.
3. The main topic of paragraph 4 is
    a. how San Francisco became the center of rock in the 1960s.
    b. the growing popularity of rock music in the 1960s.
    c. the contributions of the British to the development of rock music.
4. The last paragraph is mainly about
    a. the continuing popularity of rock music.
    b. how America is reflected in rock music.
    c. the appeal of rock music to older generations.

 ## SCANNING FOR DETAILS

Reread the passage quickly to find key words and phrases from the questions. Then write the correct answer on the line.

1. Early rock and roll was strongly influenced by _____, a dance music of African-Americans.
2. The most successful early rock and roll performer was _____.
3. _____ is considered the year that rock and roll was born.
4. The first big hit of the new style of music called rock and roll was _____ performed by _____.
5. Unlike early rock and roll, rock music of the 1960s made use of _____ and sound equipment.
6. In the 1960s, _____ was the leading center of rock music.
7. In the 1970s and early 1980s, there was great _____ progress in the production of rock music.
8. Rock music has always appealed to young people because _____.
9. _____ were the first British rock group to be successful in the United States.
10. The rock music of the late 1970s emphasized _____ and helped produce the rock styles of the 1980s and 1990s.

ORDERING EVENTS

Number the sentences to show the correct order. Do this without looking at the passage. Then reread the passage to check your answers.

_____ Synthesizers and sophisticated instruments started being used to produce rock music.

_____ The Beatles made their first hit recordings.

_____ Early rock groups began to break up.

_____ Bill Haley and His Comets performed "Rock Around the Clock."

_____ Heavy metal performers became popular.

_____ British groups like the Rolling Stones found success in the United States.

_____ Elvis Presley became the "king" of rock and roll.

 MAKING INFERENCES AND CONCLUDING

Information is not always stated directly in a passage. Sometimes we make guesses—inferences or conclusions—from the information that is in the reading. The answers to these questions are not directly stated in the passage. Circle the letter of the best answer.

1. From the passage, we can conclude that that
   a. groups outside the United States did not have much influence on rock music.
   b. rock music does not appeal to a wide audience.
   c. rock music will continue to change.

2. We can infer from the passage that
   a. rock music lost its popularity for a while in the 1970s.
   b. modern inventions had an effect on rock music.
   c. all rock music is loud and energetic.

3. The writer seems to say that
   a. rock music is not popular outside the United States.
   b. rock music was played in England before it was played in America.
   c. American culture is diverse.

DISCUSSION

Discuss the answers to the questions with your classmates.

1. What are two good or bad influences that rock music has had on people?
2. What other kinds of music do you know?
3. Who is your favorite musician or singer? Why?
4. What do you think the music of the future will be like?

WRITING

Write one or more paragraphs about ways in which young people are influenced by rock stars. Give specific details to support your ideas.

RESEARCH AND PRESENTATION

Choose a rock artist. Read about his or her life. Find the answers to the following questions.

1. Date and place of birth
2. When artist started career
3. Greatest influence on career
4. What artist is famous for

Now work with a partner or small group. Prepare a short biography of the rock artist you chose, and present it to your class. Include a photo and a recording of music performed by the artist. Be prepared to answer questions.

DID YOU KNOW . . . ?
Elvis Presley has sold over 1 billion record units worldwide, more than anyone in record industry history.

Lucas and Spielberg at the Movies

PREREADING

Answer the questions.
1. What kinds of movies do you like to see?
2. What are your favorite movies?
3. Who are your favorite movie stars?

Lucas and Spielberg at the Movies

1   The great white shark silently approaches the **unsuspecting** swimmer. The audience of *Jaws* screams in fear of the moment when those huge teeth will snap shut and pull the victim under the waves. On the screen a few years later, the **forces** of good and evil fight against each other in a faraway **galaxy** in *Star Wars.* Space people come to Earth in *Close Encounters of the Third Kind.* Later, Indiana Jones has wild adventures in *Raiders of the Lost Ark.* From outer space to the ocean's depths to imaginary treasure hunts, the movies of George Lucas and Steven Spielberg have entertained audiences for over thirty years. Moreover, these movies changed the direction of American film forever.

2   Lucas and Spielberg both achieved fame as the brightest young **talents** in Hollywood in the late 1970s and early 1980s. Two of their greatest films, *Star Wars* and *Close Encounters of the Third Kind,* appeared in the same year, 1977. Both men were nominated for an Academy Award. The two science fiction films used **special effects** that had never been seen before. Special computerized cameras were invented and miniature* models of spaceships and cities were designed. The effects on screen kept audiences breathless. When Lucas and Spielberg worked together on the action-adventure films *Raiders of the Lost Ark* and its **sequel**, *Indiana Jones and the Temple of Doom,* they once again **captured the imagination**s of the audience and made them feel as if they were a part of the action. This is what made their films so successful.

3   In a way, you can say that Steven Spielberg was a born filmmaker. He was born and grew up in Cincinnati, Ohio, and had all the interests of American boys his age. However, he also had an extraordinary desire to make films. Steven was not a good student. He spent more time watching and making movies with his father's camera than he did studying. His grades were so poor that he couldn't get into film school, so he went to study English at a state college in Los Angeles. Once again, he spent all his time going to movies. He **sneaked** onto movie sets in Hollywood to watch directors at work, and he made his own small films. One film made in 1968 called *Amblin',* which was only twenty-four minutes long, was noticed by film executives. The movie won several film awards and gave Steven his big **break**. He was signed to a seven-year contract, and at age twenty-two he became the youngest director ever to be signed to a long-term contract with a major Hollywood studio.

4   George Lucas, on the other hand, never gave a thought to making movies. Born in Modesto, California, he dreamed of being a race car driver. Three days before his high school graduation, he was in an accident that nearly killed him. He had to give up his car-racing dreams.

---

miniature: a very small copy or model of something

He went to Modesto Junior College, where he became interested in film work. A friend encouraged him and helped him get into the film department of the University of Southern California. There he made a short science fiction film that won him first prize in a film festival. When it was developed in 1967 into a full-length film, *THX 1138*, he began his career in the film business.

5   They were two very different boys with very different dreams. Lucas and Spielberg are friends today and are still among the brightest and most talented directors and producers in Hollywood. Both have made great contributions to the art of filmmaking and have become **legends** in their time. During the 1990s and beyond, they continued to produce one hit movie after another, including Spielberg's *The Lost World: Jurassic Park* in 1997 and three more of Lucas's *Star Wars* movies in 1999, 2002, and 2005. Lucas and Spielberg continue to have a great influence on American moviemaking and are sure to continue their fine work for many years to come.

VOCABULARY

 MEANING

Complete each definition with one of the following. Guess your answers, and then check them with a dictionary.

unsuspecting	galaxy	special effects	captured the imagination	break
forces	talents	sequel	sneaked	legends

1. A _____ is any large group of stars in the universe.

2. Visual or sound effects in a motion picture are _____.

3. People who have special natural abilities or skills in a particular field or area have _____.

4. A _____ to something follows as a continuation of it.

5. When someone gives you a _____, you get an unexpected chance or opportunity.

6. If a person is not aware that something is going to happen, he or she is _____.

7. People who are very famous in a particular area become _____.

8. Powers that may cause change are _____.

9. _____ is when a person went somewhere quietly and secretly without being noticed.

10. A movie that _____ kept the audience interested as if it were real.

 USE

Work with a partner to answer the questions. Use complete sentences.

1. Who are currently two big *talents* in your country?
2. In what *galaxy* is our planet Earth?
3. What is a movie that has had one *sequel*?
4. What is a book or movie that has *captured the imagination* of people in the past or present?
5. Who is a *legend* in your country?
6. In what area of your life or career would you like to get a big *break*?
7. What is a recent movie that has made great use of *special effects*?
8. What usually happens to an *unsuspecting* person?

COMPREHENSION

 SKIMMING FOR MAIN IDEAS

Quickly read to find the main idea of each paragraph, and then circle the letter of the best answer.

1. Paragraph 1 is mainly about
   a. how the movies of Lucas and Spielberg entertained audiences.
   b. how outer space adventures are popular movies with people.
   c. the importance of good and evil in movies.

2. The main topic of paragraph 2 is
   a. how Lucas and Spielberg achieved success.
   b. the two science fiction films that Lucas and Spielberg created.
   c. why special effects are important in movies.

3. The main topic of paragraph 3 is that
   a. Steven Spielberg was a poor student.
   b. Steven Spielberg was a born filmmaker.
   c. Steven Spielberg began to direct television movies.

4. Paragraph 4 is mainly about how

    a. Lucas's dream was to become a race car driver.

    b. Lucas began his career with a science fiction film.

    c. Lucas became a filmmaker by chance.

 SCANNING FOR DETAILS

Reread the passage quickly to find key words and phrases from the questions. Then circle the letter of the correct answer.

1. When George Lucas was a boy, he dreamed of becoming a

    a. race car driver.

    b. movie producer.

    c. scientist.

2. Steven Spielberg was born and grew up in

    a. Hollywood, California.

    b. Cincinnati, Ohio.

    c. Modesto, California.

3. George Lucas first became interested in film work

    a. in Hollywood.

    b. at Modesto Junior College.

    c. at the University of Southern California.

4. The forces of good and evil fight against each other in

    a. *Jaws.*

    b. *Raiders of the Lost Ark.*

    c. *Star Wars.*

5. *Star Wars* and *Close Encounters of the Third Kind* were both what kind of film?

    a. science fiction

    b. comedy

    c. drama

6. One of the things that made the films of Lucas and Spielberg so successful was

    a. good actors.

    b. special effects.

    c. interesting movie locations.

7. Steven Spielberg wasn't a good student because he spent most of his time

    a. racing cars.

    b. playing sports.

    c. making movies.

8. Lucas and Spielberg both achieved fame in the

    a. late 1970s.

    b. late 1980s.

    c. early 1990s.

9. One of the ways in which Lucas and Spielberg created special effects was by using
   a. real sharks.
   b. pictures of outer space.
   c. computerized cameras.

10. Before Spielberg became famous for his movies, he studied
    a. photography.
    b. English.
    c. computer technology.

 ORDERING EVENTS

Number the sentences to show the correct order. Do this without looking at the passage. Then reread the passage to check your answers.

_____ Lucas and Spielberg worked together on *Indiana Jones and the Temple of Doom*.

_____ George Lucas was admitted to the University of Southern California.

_____ *Raiders of the Lost Ark* was produced.

_____ Lucas and Spielberg each made their greatest films, *Star Wars* and *Close Encounters of the Third Kind*.

_____ George Lucas made the film *THX 1138*.

_____ Lucas and Spielberg were nominated for Academy Awards.

_____ Spielberg got a break with his film called *Amblin'*.

_____ Spielberg produced *The Lost World: Jurassic Park*.

 MAKING INFERENCES AND CONCLUDING

Information is not always stated directly in a passage. Sometimes we make guesses—inferences or conclusions—from the information that is in the reading. The answers to these questions are not directly stated in the passage. Circle the letter of the best answer.

1. From the passage, we can conclude that
   a. Lucas and Spielberg both showed promise as filmmakers in their youth.
   b. Spielberg became a filmmaker because he couldn't do anything else.
   c. Lucas and Spielberg have had a major influence on today's films.

2. We can infer from the passage that
   a. Lucas and Spielberg followed traditional ways of filmmaking.
   b. the types of films Lucas and Spielberg made in the 1980s would not be popular today.
   c. Lucas and Spielberg are both highly creative individuals.

3. The writer seems to say that

    a. science fiction films are more popular than action-adventure films.

    b. audiences like to feel as if they are part of the action.

    c. audiences don't like to be frightened by movies.

DISCUSSION

Discuss the answers to the questions with your classmates.

1. Do you prefer to go out to the movies or to watch a video at home? Why?
2. Do you like movies with special effects? Why?
3. Which type of movie do you like best? Why?
4. Who are some famous filmmakers in your country? What kinds of movies do they make?

WRITING

Think about your favorite movie. Write two to three paragraphs about it. Tell the story, and give reasons why you like it.

RESEARCH AND PRESENTATION

The following are names of famous film directors and producers. Find the names of two movies they are famous for.

1. Francis Ford Coppola
2. Michael Douglas
3. Clint Eastwood
4. Alfred Hitchcock
5. Kevin Costner
6. Robert Redford

Now work with a partner or small group. Prepare a short biography of one of these people for your class. Provide photos. Give examples of their films. Be prepared to answer questions.

DID YOU KNOW . . . ?
George Lucas wrote the entire original script for *Star Wars* by hand, in tiny printing, with sharp No. 2 pencils.

Television Comes to America

PREREADING

Answer the questions.

1. How many hours of television do you watch every day?
2. What TV programs do you like to watch? Why?
3. What is the most popular television program in your country?

Television Comes to America

1   One of the greatest influences on life in modern America has been television. It affects how Americans dress, talk, and relax. It influences how they vote and view themselves and others. It is one of the most important and powerful inventions of all time.

2   Many Americans can't imagine life without television. Yet television didn't become part of the average American household until the 1950s. As early as 1879, scientists were looking for ways to add pictures to sound. Inventors worldwide experimented with many types of picture machines. One was called *radio vision*. It used **spinning disks** to transmit pictures. Then in 1922, a fourteen-year-old American farm boy named Philo T. Farnsworth thought of using electricity **to scan** and transmit pictures.

3   Farnsworth was born in 1906 in a cabin near Beaver, Utah. He worked on his father's farm when he wasn't in school. He was an imaginative boy and very interested in science, especially electricity. When he was still in high school, Farnsworth began experimenting with the idea of using glass tubes and electricity to transmit sound and pictures. After he graduated from college, someone gave him money for one year while he experimented with his idea for television. Just three weeks before the year was over, Farnsworth produced his first TV picture. In 1930, at the age of twenty-four, he **was granted** the first electronic television **patent**.

4   Most major inventions take the combined efforts of many scientists and inventors. In the case of television, a Russian-American named Vladimir Zworykin invented and patented the eye of the television camera and the television screen. For that reason, Zworykin and Farnsworth share the title of "The Fathers of Modern Television."

5   The first televisions were very expensive and still had some problems. Few people had them, and broadcasting was extremely limited. But by 1945 television sets were **rolling off** the **assembly lines**. The big radio broadcasting networks began producing funny and entertaining television shows. News shows were informative. People watched TV in store windows and at the homes of neighbors who were lucky enough to own a television.

6   Soon everyone was saving up to buy a TV. In the beginning of 1950, there were 3 million television sets in the United States. By the end of the year there were 7 million sets. By 1951, some young people were watching nearly thirty hours of television a week! Television became a **craze**, and people couldn't get enough of it. They even started eating meals in front of the television. From this habit, frozen "TV dinners" and "TV trays" to put them on were born in 1954.

7   Television influenced people so strongly that they copied what they saw and heard. In 1955, a Disney film about the frontiersman Davy Crockett

was shown. Children and adults loved it. Soon everyone was singing "Davy, Davy Crockett, king of the wild frontier." Everything from pencils to school lunchboxes had a picture of Davy Crockett on it. Experts began to worry that children were watching too much television, and that it was influencing everyone too easily. Many predicted it would destroy the American family and way of life. However, the average person didn't care what the experts thought. People loved television and wanted more of it.

8   Today, most American families have at least two TV sets. The only activity that takes up more of their free time is sleeping. Some experts still criticize them for the amount of time they spend in front of the television, but Americans have also proved they are interested in more than entertainment. One of the largest daytime TV audiences in history watched on May 5, 1961, as astronaut Alan Shepard became the first American to take off into space. In 1969, approximately 600 million people worldwide watched astronaut Neil Armstrong take the first step on the moon.

9   Although Americans like to be entertained, they are also **eager** to be informed. The variety of television programming has expanded greatly over the years. Television has proved it can be a wonderful tool for education. Many stations only show programs on nature, science, music, language, and other educational subjects. News stations keep people informed twenty-four hours a day. Busy Americans can shop through home-shopping networks, and sports enthusiasts can watch all their favorite games and players.

10   The **pace** of new technology is the only thing that limits the future of television. Sharper images, smaller "boxes," bigger and bigger screens, surround sound, screens within screens, stop action, and many other features are all part of our present technology. It will only continue to improve. Many televisions are **linked to** computers today, but improvements in wireless technology will soon connect all TVs to computers, telephones, cell phones, notebooks, and all kinds of handheld devices. Learning, shopping, banking, communicating, and entertaining will all be functions of television. Viewers will have more choices and opportunities than ever. They'll choose what programs they want and when to watch them. They won't even have to use their remote controls. The televisions of tomorrow will have voice command. Just think. After all these years that televisions have been talking to us, we'll finally have an opportunity to talk back!

VOCABULARY

 MEANING

Complete each definition with one of the following. Guess your answers, and then check them with a dictionary.

spinning disks	was granted	rolling off	craze	pace
to scan	patent	assembly line	eager	linked to

1. The speed or the rate of movement of something is its _____.
2. Something connected to something else is _____ it.
3. When a person is full of interest or desire, he or she is _____.
4. When something becomes fashionable, it is a _____.
5. A document from a government office that gives someone the right to make or sell a new invention is called a _____.
6. To put an object under a moving electron beam that converts it to an image that can be transmitted is _____.
7. When something requested was given, it _____.
8. An _____ is a series of work stations for certain steps required to make a specific product.
9. _____ are thin circular objects that revolve very rapidly.
10. When products are _____ an assembly line, they are being manufactured quickly and in large quantities.

 USE

Work with a partner to answer the questions. Use complete sentences.

1. What is one product that is built on an *assembly line*?
2. What is one thing that you wish *was granted* to you?
3. What is currently a *craze*?
4. What is a product that is *rolling off* assembly lines in great numbers today?
5. What is something you are *eager* to have or do?
6. If you could invent *something* and get a *patent*, what would it be?
7. What is an object that is made with things *linked to* each other?
8. What is one technology that is changing at a rapid *pace* today?

COMPREHENSION

 SKIMMING FOR MAIN IDEAS

Quickly read to find the main idea of each paragraph, and then circle the letter of the best answer.

1. The main topic of paragraph 3 is about how
   a. Farnsworth was interested in inventions.
   b. Farnsworth produced his first television picture.
   c. the first television patent was given to Farnsworth.
2. Paragraph 7 is mainly about
   a. the influence television had on children and the family.
   b. the popularity of the film *Davy Crockett*.
   c. the experts' warnings that children watched too much television.
3. The main topic of paragraph 9 is
   a. home-shopping networks on television.
   b. television as a tool for education.
   c. the variety of programs on television.
4. The main topic of the last paragraph is that
   a. future television will have a variety of functions.
   b. televisions will have voice command in the future.
   c. televisions will be linked to computers.

 SCANNING FOR DETAILS

Reread the passage quickly to find key words and phrases from the questions. Then write the correct answer on the line.

1. "The Fathers of Modern Television" are _____ and
   _____.
2. When Farnsworth was a high school student, he experimented with using
   _____ and _____ to transmit _____
   and _____.
3. Very few people had the first televisions available because they were
   _____ and _____.
4. When people started eating meals in front of the television, it led to the
   invention of _____ and _____.

5. Television can be used for _____, as well as entertainment.

6. One of the most popular films in 1955 was about _____.

7. Experts warned that TV might hurt _____ and

   _____.

8. Most American families have at least _____ TV sets.

9. Televisions will continue to improve with new _____.

10. Televisions and _____ will work together in the future and become part of the "information superhighway."

⭐ ORDERING EVENTS

Number the sentences to show the correct order. Do this without looking at the passage. Then reread the passage to check your answers.

_____ Farnsworth was given money to experiment with television for a year.

_____ Radio vision was invented.

_____ Americans started doing their shopping by using home-shopping networks on TV.

_____ Six hundred million viewers watched Neil Armstrong step onto the moon.

_____ Farnsworth was granted a patent for his television.

_____ Farnsworth graduated from college.

_____ There were 3 million television sets in the United States.

⭐ MAKING INFERENCES AND CONCLUDING

Information is not always stated directly in a passage. Sometimes we make guesses—inferences or conclusions—from the information that is in the reading. The answers to these questions are not directly stated in the passage. Circle the letter of the best answer.

1. From the passage, we can conclude that
   a. television was an invention in which people saw only advantages.
   b. it took Americans a long time to begin to appreciate the invention of television.
   c. the invention of television had an effect on American customs.

2. We can infer from the passage that
    a. television has developed primarily into a tool for education.
    b. Americans like to have a variety of programs to choose from.
    c. programs showing people traveling into space are the most popular programs on television today.
3. The writer seems to say that
    a. television will continue to expand its usefulness in the future.
    b. Americans are more interested in watching television than in sleeping.
    c. television programming can't keep up with the development of new technology.

DISCUSSION

Discuss the answers to the questions with your classmates.

1. How do you think television has affected family life?
2. How do you think violence on television affects people?
3. If you could decide what is shown on TV, what kinds of programs would you broadcast?
4. What are some of the advantages and disadvantages of combining TV with computers?

WRITING

Write one or more paragraphs that explain at least two reasons for or against watching television. Be sure to support you reasons with specific details.

RESEARCH AND PRESENTATION

Find out what communication device each of the following people invented, the year it was invented, and in what country.

1. John Logie Baird
2. Alexander Graham Bell
3. Chester Carlson
4. Johannes Gutenberg
5. Arthur Korn
6. Samuel Morse

Now work with a partner or small group. Prepare a presentation that explains one invention and why it is or was important. Describe the invention and show pictures. Be prepared to answer questions.

DID YOU KNOW . . . ?

By nineteen years of age, the typical U.S. young person has spent about 25,000 hours watching television, which is actually more time than is spent learning in school.

UNIT 24

Hip-Hop Culture

PREREADING

Answer the questions.

1. Do you like songs about people's struggles in life? Why?
2. What famous rap musicians do you know?
3. Do you like rap music? Why?

Hip-Hop Culture

1   Hip-hop is a culture that began in the early 1970s in a part of New York City called the Bronx. It was created by African-American youth as a way to fully express themselves, so the hip-hop lifestyle includes music, dance, speech, art, and fashion. Specifically, it includes rap music, breakdancing, talking slang,* graffiti art, and dressing in baggy clothes. Over its nearly forty years of existence, hip-hop has moved from a single area and a small group to influence an entire generation across the globe.

2   A Jamaican immigrant named Clive Campbell, who took the name Kool Herc, is the originator of hip-hop music, also known as rap. Campbell moved from Jamaica to New York in 1967 at the age of twelve. He brought with him a music style called "toasting." At dances and parties in Jamaica in the 1950s, 1960s, and 1970s, there was always a "deejay," the person who played the music. In between playing the records, and sometimes while the record was playing, the deejay told stories and jokes to the audience and called out to them to enjoy themselves.

3   In the early 1970s, Kool Herc practiced toasting, and after a while he created a new sound, using American music. He also built his own **sound system** with huge speakers. He would play music and shout out to the audience lines like, "Yes, yes, y'all. You're listening to the sound of . . . I just want to say to all my B-boys . . . boys . . . oys . . . Rock on!" After a while he had other boys—MCs—do the announcing while he made the music. These announcers told stories, greeted the audience, asked them questions, and encouraged everyone to dance and sing. The MCs spoke in rhythm to the music, and this became known as rapping.

4   Meanwhile, Kool Herc was creating new music sounds by taking parts of songs and music and putting them together. Other artists in the area, such as Grandmaster Flash and Afrika Bambaataa, created their own sounds and experimented with new ways of putting together different sounds and types of music. In 1982, Afrika Bambaataa's *Planet Rock* became the first hip-hop record to use synthesizers and electronic drums.

5   Hip-hop music was played mostly at huge parties on neighborhood streets. While records were changed and during breaks in the music played on records, people began to dance in a style that became known as breakdancing. Breakdancing **involved** all kinds of moves, including fast footwork, dancing on one's hands, spinning on one's head, kicking, falling, and other moves. Breakdancers wore low baggy pants, big T-shirts, a hat worn to the side, and sneakers—what then became hip-hop fashion.

6   While breakdancing was the physical expression of rap music, graffiti art became a **visual** expression of it. Graffiti has actually existed as long as

---

slang: special words that are not part of standard language and are spoken by people who do the same work or have the same way of life, usually not understood by outsiders

humans have been writing on walls, ancient and otherwise. Graffiti means "writing on the wall." However, modern graffiti is known as writing on public surfaces with spray paint and **markers**, and is usually illegal. Graffiti is done in bright colors and shows off the artists' nicknames in large letters that flow into one another. These nicknames are known as "tags." The first hip-hop graffiti artists took names such as Taki 183, Super Kool 223, Crash, and Daze. Graffiti artists competed to make their names known on the subway systems of New York City. In the 1980s, cities began to **wage wars** against graffiti, making surfaces on which paint wouldn't stick or painting over graffiti as quickly as possible. However, they still haven't **won that battle**.

7   During the mid-1980s, hip-hop moved from the African-American neighborhoods to areas across America and through the music industry. Hip-hop artists such as Run-DMC, Heavy D, and LL Cool J began to tour the country. Salt-N-Pepa became the first well-known female hip-hop group. By the late 1980s, new hip-hop styles began to appear, such as political rap, jazz rap, and gangsta rap.

8   In the 1990s, gangsta rap grew in popularity with artists like Snoop Doggy Dogg, Ice Cube, and Ice-T. It spoke of the lifestyle of **hardship**, drugs, and violence in inner-city America. Through gangsta rap, African-American youth talked about the world around them and how they felt about it, but their violent lyrics were controversial. A lot of people criticized rap as encouraging violence, drug use, and mistreatment of women. Many rap artists argued that their **lyrics** simply talked about reality to people who understood what it was like.

9   Gangsta rap is still very popular, but it is only one style of rap. Other rappers have provided positive messages about **self-help**, respect, pride, and improvement. In the 1990s, there was an artistic and poetic movement led by De la Soul, A Tribe Called Quest, Queen Latifah, and others.

10   Hip-hop is constantly changing and adding new styles and subjects, and today, two out of every ten records sold in America is hip-hop. It is enjoyed, performed, and **imitated** across the world. From a neighborhood lifestyle, it has become a global movement and will probably live on in one form or another for many years to come.

VOCABULARY

⭐ MEANING

What is the meaning of the underlined words? Circle the letter of the correct answer. Use a dictionary to check your answers.

1. He built his own <u>sound system</u>.
   a. a collection of songs
   b. a set of recorders
   c. a group of speakers

2. Breakdancing <u>involved</u> all kinds of moves.
   a. caused or made
   b. contained or included
   c. went in circles around

3. Graffiti art is a <u>visual</u> expression of hip-hop.
   a. something that can be heard
   b. something that can be seen
   c. something that can be felt

4. Graffiti artists use spray paint and <u>markers</u>.
   a. tools used for putting lines on a surface
   b. devices used for shaping solid figures
   c. instruments used to cut objects

5. Cities began to <u>wage wars</u> against graffiti.
   a. cause fights
   b. end battles
   c. carry on fights

6. They still haven't <u>won that battle</u>.
   a. succeeded in achieving a goal
   b. ended a long journey
   c. started an assignment

7. Gangsta rap speaks of the <u>hardship</u> of life in the inner city.
   a. hard work
   b. old ways of life
   c. difficult conditions

8. Rap artists say that their <u>lyrics</u> are about reality.
   a. music to a song
   b. singers of a song
   c. words of a song

9. Some rappers express messages about <u>self-help</u>.
   a. doing something on one's own to improve oneself
   b. asking others for help with something
   c. doing something to improve the lives of other people

10. Hip-hop is <u>imitated</u> around the world.
    a. copied
    b. liked
    c. played

USE

Work with a partner to answer the questions. Use complete sentences.

1. What are some of the *lyrics* to your favorite song?
2. What is something American that is *imitated* in other countries?
3. What is a place that has a large *sound system*?
4. What is a dance style in your country that has always *involved* difficult steps or movements?
5. What is a *hardship* experienced by people in poor areas of your country?
6. What are some things you can do with *markers*?
7. What is one of the *visual* arts?
8. What kind of *self-help* books can be found at your local bookstore?

COMPREHENSION

 SKIMMING FOR MAIN IDEAS

Quickly read to find the main idea of each paragraph, and then circle the letter of the best answer.

1. Paragraph 1 is mainly about
   a. how hip-hop got started in New York City.
   b. what the elements of hip-hop are.
   c. how hip-hop grew to have a global influence.
2. The main topic of paragraph 3 is
   a. the kind of music Kool Herc played.
   b. where rapping came from.
   c. how Kool Herc built his own sound system.
3. The main topic of paragraph 6 is
   a. the history of graffiti.
   b. the battle between graffiti artists and city authorities.
   c. the characteristics of modern graffiti.
4. Paragraph 8 is mainly about
   a. various opinions about gangsta rap.
   b. the hardships of life in inner-city America.
   c. the popularity of gangsta rap.

⭐ SCANNING FOR DETAILS

Reread the passage quickly to find key words and phrases from the questions. Circle *T* if the sentence is true. Circle *F* if the sentence is false.

1. Music, dance, language, art, and dress are all part of hip-hop culture. T F
2. Hip-hop culture began in African-American neighborhoods of New York City. T F
3. In Jamaican "toasting," a deejay called out to the audience and told jokes and stories. T F
4. Early rapping was done by musicians who used different kinds of musical instruments. T F
5. *Planet Rock* was the first hip-hop record to put together parts of different songs and music. T F
6. Breakdancing was done mostly on stage at big dances. T F
7. Graffiti means "writing on the wall." T F
8. Graffiti showed scenes of hardship in the city. T F
9. The first famous female hip-hop group was Salt-N-Pepa. T F
10. Gangsta rap was too controversial to be popular. T F

⭐ ORDERING EVENTS

Number the sentences to show the correct order. Do this without looking at the passage. Then reread the passage to check your answers.

_____ The hip-hop sound and culture move out of African-American communities and spread across America.

_____ *Planet Rock* becomes the first hip-hop record to use synthesizers.

_____ Kool Herc practices Jamaican toasting techniques and creates a new form of music.

_____ Artists create new music sounds by experimenting with ways of putting together music.

_____ Clive Campbell moves to New York from Jamaica.

_____ Snoop Doggy Dogg, Ice Cube, and Ice-T help to make gangsta rap popular.

_____ Deejays in Jamaica tell stories and call out to audiences in a style called "toasting."

⭐ MAKING INFERENCES AND CONCLUDING

Information is not always stated directly in a passage. Sometimes we make guesses—inferences or conclusions—from the information that is in the reading. The answers to these questions are not directly stated in the passage. Circle the letter of the best answer.

1. From the passage, we can conclude that
   a. because hip-hop was an expression of African-American life, it wasn't understood by people outside of black communities.
   b. hip-hop had meaning beyond African-American culture and touched lives everywhere.
   c. rap music didn't play a big part in the popularization of hip-hop culture.

2. The writer seems to say that
   a. when hip-hop spread across the country, it no longer had meaning for members of the African-American communities.
   b. hip-hop was a culture that most black youths could not understand.
   c. hip-hop gave people who were struggling an opportunity to express themselves.

3. We can infer from the passage that hip-hop culture
   a. sometimes went against traditional rules and laws.
   b. was all about violence and negative things in life.
   c. has been unable to change with the times and will eventually fade away.

DISCUSSION

Discuss the answers to the questions with your classmates.

1. What kind of music is native to your country?
2. Is there any music in your country that is controversial? Why is it controversial?
3. Why do you think hip-hop became so popular around the world?
4. Do you think graffiti is art? Why? Is graffiti a problem in your country? Where?

WRITING

Some people say that rap isn't really music. What is your opinion?
Do you think that "real" music can only be played with traditional
instruments and singing styles? Do you think that young people should
be allowed to listen to rap? Write one or more paragraphs that give your
opinions about these questions. Be sure to include specific reasons that
support your opinion.

RESEARCH AND PRESENTATION

Choose a type of music, such as blues, jazz, country, soul, R&B, punk,
or heavy metal. Read about it and find the answers to the following
questions.

1. When and where did the music
   style get started?

2. What kind of instruments are
   used to play it?

3. What are two important
   characteristics of the music?

4. Who is a famous performer or
   group that plays the music?

Now work with a partner or small group. Prepare a short presentation
about one type of music. Include information from your research and a
recording of the music. Be prepared to answer questions.

DID YOU KNOW . . . ?
The British buy the most compact discs (CDs) in the world—an average of
3.2 per person per year, compared to 2.8 in the United States and 2.1 in France.

ANSWER KEY

UNIT 1

VOCABULARY: MEANING
1. clogged   2. a flat tire   3. expanded
4. clouds of dust   5. windshields   6. decades
7. speaker   8. courtyard   9. diners   10. at its height

USE
Answers will vary.

COMPREHENSION: SKIMMING FOR MAIN IDEAS
1. a   2. c   3. c   4. b

SCANNING FOR DETAILS
1. c   2. b   3. b   4. c   5. a   6. a   7. c   8. a
9. b   10. a

ORDERING EVENTS
5, 4, 1, 3, 6, 2, 7

MAKING INFERENCES AND CONCLUDING
1. a   2. a   3. c

UNIT 2

VOCABULARY: MEANING
1. a   2. c   3. b   4. c   5. a   6. a   7. b
8. b   9. a   10. c

USE
Answers will vary.

COMPREHENSION: SKIMMING FOR MAIN IDEAS
1. b   2. a   3. a   4. c

SCANNING FOR DETAILS
1.   the river froze
2.   work with him in his tobacco shop
3.   the tallest ships to pass under it
4.   two towers
5.   it was sand and mud
6.   dig out dirt and rocks
7.   the weight of the water against it
8.   she was a woman
9.   string the huge cables between them
10.   14

ORDERING EVENTS
3, 5, 7, 1, 4, 2, 6

MAKING INFERENCES AND CONCLUDING
1. b   2. c   3. a

SOME INTERESTING FACTS
Before the roadway was built, there was a wooden footbridge for the workers to use. The views from the footbridge were incredible. Soon, everyone was talking about it. Tourists started coming to walk on it. The footbridge was narrow and it rocked in the wind. Over a hundred feet below, the river rushed past. For some, it was an exciting experience, but for others it was frightening. Some people panicked, and others fainted and had to be carried off the footbridge. Eventually it was closed to the public.

There are 5,434 wires in each main cable.

Total length of the roadway is 5,989 feet.

Height of the roadway above the water in the center of river is 135 feet.

UNIT 3

VOCABULARY: MEANING
1. soundtracks   2. leaned forward
3. versatile   4. dropped out
5. inspirational   6. way ahead
7. rebellious   8. exceptional
9. touch the hearts   10. universal

USE
Answers will vary.

COMPREHENSION: SKIMMING FOR MAIN IDEAS
1. b   2. b   3. c   4. c

SCANNING FOR DETAILS

1.	~~London~~	Paris
2.	~~doctors~~	musicians
3.	~~three-stringed~~	four-stringed
4.	~~seven~~	eight
5.	~~Columbia~~	Harvard
6.	~~Africa~~	Argentina
7.	~~told people not to take taxis in New York~~	reminded passengers to take their belongings with them
8.	~~Los Angeles~~	Long Island, New York

9. ~~legs~~ spine
10. ~~Europe and America~~ 10 different countries around the world

ORDERING EVENTS
3, 1, 6, 4, 5, 2

MAKING INFERENCES AND CONCLUDING
1. b   2. b   3. a

UNIT 4

VOCABULARY: MEANING
1. b   2. a   3. c   4. a   5. b   6. a   7. b
8. c   9. c   10. a

USE
Answers will vary.

COMPREHENSION: SKIMMING FOR MAIN IDEAS
1. a   2. a   3. b   4. c

SCANNING FOR DETAILS
1. ~~dark red~~ white
2. ~~voices~~ spirits
3. ~~friends~~ babies
4. ~~alone~~ in packs
5. ~~three year old~~ parents
6. ~~anger~~ excitement or happiness
7. ~~raising the young~~ hunting
8. ~~several females~~ a male and female
9. ~~use up the food supply~~ keep the balance of nature
10. ~~usually~~ never OR ~~healthy~~ sick or weak

ORDERING EVENTS
5, 4, 1, 6, 2, 3

MAKING INFERENCES AND CONCLUDING
1. c   2. a   3. b

UNIT 5

VOCABULARY: MEANING
1. amphibians   2. burrows   3. searing
4. salt flats   5. harsh   6. devoid of   7. shrubs
8. pioneers   9. precious   10. lodged

USE
Answers will vary.

COMPREHENSION: SKIMMING FOR MAIN IDEAS
1. a   2. a   3. b   4. c

SCANNING FOR DETAILS
1. c   2. a   3. c   4. b   5. a   6. a   7. b
8. b   9. c   10. b

ORDERING EVENTS
4, 6, 2, 3, 7, 5, 8, 1

MAKING INFERENCES AND CONCLUDING
1. a   2. c   3. c

UNIT 6

VOCABULARY: MEANING
1. chip   2. abundant   3. trunk   4. aroma   5. tedious
6. clusters   7. grove   8. nourishing   9. cultivated
10. spouts

USE
Answers will vary.

COMPREHENSION: SKIMMING FOR MAIN IDEAS
1. b   2. b   3. a   4. b

SCANNING FOR DETAILS
1. mokuks
2. sugar
3. 100 feet
4. the meat of the pecan is rich and nourishing
5. central southern United States
6. days are warm and nights are cold
7. tapping
8. boiled
9. 75 to 100
10. 25 to 30 gallons

ORDERING EVENTS
6, 4, 1, 3, 2, 5

MAKING INFERENCES AND CONCLUDING
1. b   2. a   3. b

UNIT 7

VOCABULARY: MEANING
1. b   2. c   3. b   4. a   5. c   6. a   7. b
8. a   9. c   10. b

USE
Answers will vary.

COMPREHENSION: SKIMMING FOR MAIN IDEAS
1. b   2. a   3. c   4. a

SCANNING FOR DETAILS
1. Milwaukee, Wisconsin
2. read and write
3. seven
4. a special center for troubled girls
5. celebrities
6. her father or Vernon Winfrey
7. *The Color Purple* and *Native Son*
8. Tennessee State University
9. news show anchor
10. witty, charming, warm

ORDERING EVENTS
7, 3, 1, 4, 5, 2, 6

MAKING INFERENCES AND CONCLUDING
1. b   2. b   3. b

UNIT 8

VOCABULARY: MEANING
1. b   2. a   3. a   4. b   5. b   6. b   7. a
8. c   9. a   10. a

USE
Answers will vary.

COMPREHENSION: SKIMMING FOR MAIN IDEAS
1. b   2. c   3. a   4. b

SCANNING FOR DETAILS
1. T   2. F   3. T   4. F   5. F   6. F   7. T
8. T   9. T   10. F

ORDERING EVENTS
7, 2, 6, 1, 8, 4, 3, 5

MAKING INFERENCES AND CONCLUDING
1. c   2. c   3. a

UNIT 9

VOCABULARY: MEANING
1. b   2. a   3. c   4. b   5. b   6. a   7. b
8. c   9. a   10. a

USE
Answers will vary.

COMPREHENSION: SKIMMING FOR MAIN IDEAS
1. c   2. a   3. b   4. b

SCANNING FOR DETAILS
1. ~~accurate~~   wrong
2. ~~single-wing airship~~   double-wing glider
3. ~~motorcycle~~   bicycle
4. ~~South Carolina~~   North Carolina
5. ~~bought~~   built
6. ~~straightening~~   bending
7. ~~a cockpit~~   straighter wings
                           and a rudder
8. ~~10 seconds and   12 seconds and
   200 feet~~   120 feet
9. ~~America~~   Europe
10. ~~crowd~~   small group

ORDERING EVENTS
3, 1, 4, 5, 6, 2, 7

MAKING INFERENCES AND CONCLUDING
1. c   2. a   3. c

UNIT 10

VOCABULARY: MEANING
1. c   2. a   3. c   4. a   5. b   6. b   7. b
8. a   9. a   10. a

USE
Answers will vary.

COMPREHENSION: SKIMMING FOR MAIN IDEAS
1. a   2. b   3. b   4. a

SCANNING FOR DETAILS
1. T   2. T   3. F   4. F   5. F   6. F   7. F
8. T   9. F   10. F

ORDERING EVENTS
4, 6, 1, 3, 7, 2, 5

MAKING INFERENCES AND CONCLUDING
1. a   2. c   3. c

UNIT 11

VOCABULARY: MEANING
1. c   2. b   3. c   4. b   5. b   6. c   7. a
8. a   9. b   10. c

USE
Answers will vary.

COMPREHENSION: SKIMMING FOR MAIN IDEAS
1. c   2. c   3. b   4. b

SCANNING FOR DETAILS

1. skateboarding
2. roller skates
3. they couldn't go surfing in the water
4. urethane wheels
5. a type of small Olympics for extreme sports
6. sailing and surfing
7. 1984
8. rope
9. new designs
10. couldn't control their boards and would cause accidents

ORDERING EVENTS

3, 6, 1, 8, 5, 7, 4, 2

MAKING INFERENCES AND CONCLUDING

1. c   2. c   3. a

UNIT 12

VOCABULARY: MEANING

1. b   2. a   3. c   4. c   5. b   6. a   7. b
8. c   9. a   10. a

USE

Answers will vary.

COMPREHENSION: SKIMMING FOR MAIN IDEAS

1. b   2. b   3. c   4. a

SCANNING FOR DETAILS

1. F   2. T   3. F   4. T   5. F   6. F   7. T
8. T   9. F   10. T

ORDERING EVENTS

5, 1, 6, 3, 8, 2, 7, 4

MAKING INFERENCES AND CONCLUDING

1. a   2. a   3. c

UNIT 13

VOCABULARY: MEANING

1. troops   2. give up   3. was arrested   4. social events
5. set up   6. trial   7. authorities   8. adopted by
9. run by   10. prosperous

USE

Answers will vary.

COMPREHENSION: SKIMMING FOR MAIN IDEAS

1. b   2. a   3. b   4. c

SCANNING FOR DETAILS

1. b   2. a   3. c   4. a   5. c   6. b   7. c
8. b   9. a   10. c

ORDERING EVENTS

3, 6, 4, 1, 5, 2

MAKING INFERENCES AND CONCLUDING

1. c   2. a   3. c

UNIT 14

VOCABULARY: MEANING

1. timber   2. eccentric   3. on record
4. vast   5. reefs   6. thaws   7. mosses
8. mountain range   9. spectacular
10. natural phenomenon

USE

Answers will vary.

COMPREHENSION: SKIMMING FOR MAIN IDEAS

1. b   2. a   3. c   4. a

SCANNING FOR DETAILS

1. Great Land, Aleut
2. Kodiak
3. tundra
4. The Land of the Midnight Sun
5. native peoples; descendants of early settlers
6. Mt. Mc Kinley; 20, 320
7. Northern Lights; Aurora Borealis
8. 100,000; 3,000
9. airplane; much of Alaska doesn't have roads.
10. Siberia

ORDERING EVENTS

6, 2, 1, 4, 5, 3

MAKING INFERENCES AND CONCLUDING

1. b   2. c   3. b

UNIT 15

VOCABULARY: MEANING

1. stamina   2. frigid   3. kennel
4. sled dog team   5. skidded off
6. rigorous   7. trail   8. grueling
9. untangled   10. desperately

USE

Answers will vary.

COMPREHENSION: SKIMMING FOR MAIN IDEAS

1. a   2. b   3. c   4. a

SCANNING FOR DETAILS

1.	~~3,000~~	1,000
2.	~~1940~~	1925
3.	~~went to college to become a veterinarian~~	began to train and run dogs for a racing kennel
4.	~~ten~~	twenty
5.	~~they couldn't find a pilot~~	it was too stormy
6.	~~bear~~	moose
7.	~~1987~~	1988
8.	~~someone offered her a job~~	reading about the Iditarod in a magazine
9.	~~first~~	second
10.	~~the doctor who sent for the medicine~~	one of the towns it passes through

ORDERING EVENTS

4, 6, 2, 1, 7, 3, 5

MAKING INFERENCES AND CONCLUDING

1. b   2. a   3. a

UNIT 16

VOCABULARY: MEANING

1. collapsible   2. lunar   3. living quarters   4. gravity
5. barren   6. set foot in   7. ferries   8. rugged
9. craft   10. drifted

USE

Answers will vary.

COMPREHENSION: SKIMMING FOR MAIN IDEAS

1. a   2. c   3. b   4. b

SCANNING FOR DETAILS

1. Giovanni Riccioli; telescope
2. lunar rover; moon buggy
3. the Sea of Tranquilty
4. Apollo 17
5. gray rock and soil
6. moon base
7. 212 degrees Farenheit, boil water
8. there is no air
9. six times less
10. it was damaged by an explosion

ORDERING EVENTS

3, 6, 1, 4, 2, 5

MAKING INFERENCES AND CONCLUDING

1. c   2. a   3. b

UNIT 17

VOCABULARY: MEANING

1. a   2. b   3. c   4. c   5. b   6. b   7. c
8. a   9. a   10. c

USE

Answers will vary.

COMPREHENSION: SKIMMING FOR MAIN IDEAS

1. a   2. b   3. a   4. c

SCANNING FOR DETAILS

1. Kansas State University
2. 12; Mc Neil Island
3. canaries or birds
4. engineering; music; mathematics
5. third-grade
6. all of his belongings or things
7. mother; President Wilson (and his wife)
8. on a rocky island in San Francisco Bay
9. life in solitary confinement
10. diseases of birds

ORDERING EVENTS

3, 2, 6, 1, 5, 7, 4

MAKING INFERENCES AND CONCLUDING

1. a   2. b   3. a

UNIT 18

VOCABULARY: MEANING

1. on a mission   2. has been around   3. figures
4. got trapped   5. come to life   6. pad
7. contribution   8. hit   9. track   10. image

USE

Answers will vary.

COMPREHENSION: SKIMMING FOR MAIN IDEAS

1. b   2. b   3. c   4. a

SCANNING FOR DETAILS

1.	~~animated~~	computer generated
2.	~~board~~	reel
3.	~~different figure~~	figure with a slight change
4.	~~long lengths~~	clear sheets
5.	~~image~~	figure
6.	~~Earl Hurd~~	Walt Disney

7. ~~a computer~~
    ~~screen~~   an electronic
                       drawing pad
8. ~~animated figures~~   special effects
9. ~~voices~~   looks and movements
10. ~~movies~~   computer animation

ORDERING EVENTS
6, 8, 2, 5, 7, 1, 3, 4

MAKING INFERENCES AND CONCLUDING
1. c   2. b   3. b

UNIT 19

VOCABULARY: MEANING
1. b   2. a   3. b   4. a   5. c   6. c   7. b
8. a   9. a   10. c

USE
Answers will vary.

COMPREHENSION: SKIMMING FOR MAIN IDEAS
1. c   2. b   3. b   4. a

SCANNING FOR DETAILS
1. F   2. F   3. T   4. T   5. T   6. F   7. F
8. T   9. F   10. T

ORDERING EVENTS
6, 3, 5, 1, 7, 4, 2

MAKING INFERENCES AND CONCLUDING
1. a   2. c   3. c

UNIT 20

VOCABULARY: MEANING
1. contact sport   2. extravaganza   3. to ban
4. opponent's   5. substituted for   6. squads   7. floats
8. banners   9. drills   10. strategy

USE
Answers will vary.

COMPREHENSION: SKIMMING FOR MAIN IDEAS
1. a   2. b   3. c   4. c

SCANNING FOR DETAILS
1. c   2. b   3. b   4. c   5. a   6. c   7. b
8. a   9. c   10. a

ORDERING EVENTS
2, 4, 8, 6, 7, 3, 1, 5

MAKING INFERENCES AND CONCLUDING
1. b   2. c   3. a

UNIT 21

VOCABULARY: MEANING
1. c   2. b   3. c   4. a   5. a   6. c   7. b
8. c   9. a   10. c

USE
Answers will vary.

COMPREHENSION: SKIMMING FOR MAIN IDEAS
1. b   2. b   3. c   4. a

SCANNING FOR DETAILS
1. rhythm and blues
2. Elvis Presley
3. 1955
4. *Rock Around the Clock*, Bill Haley and His Comets
5. electronic instruments
6. San Francisco
7. technological
8. it's an expression of their search for identity and independence
9. the Beatles
10. rhythm and energy

ORDERING EVENTS
7, 4, 6, 1, 3, 5, 2

MAKING INFERENCES AND CONCLUDING
1. c   2. b   3. c

UNIT 22

VOCABULARY: MEANING
1. galaxy   2. special effects   3. talents
4. sequel   5. break   6. unsuspecting
7. legends   8. forces   9. sneaked
10. captured the imagination

USE
Answers will vary.

COMPREHENSION: SKIMMING FOR MAIN IDEAS
1. a   2. a   3. b   4. c

SCANNING FOR DETAILS
1. a   2. b   3. b   4. c   5. a   6. b   7. c
8. a   9. c   10. b

ORDERING EVENTS
7, 1, 6, 4, 2, 5, 3, 8

MAKING INFERENCES AND CONCLUDING
1. c   2. c   3. b

UNIT 23

VOCABULARY: MEANING
1. pace   2. linked to   3. eager   4. craze
5. patent   6. to scan   7. was granted
8. assembly line   9. spinning disks
10. rolling off

USE
Answers will vary.

COMPREHENSION: SKIMMING FOR MAIN IDEAS
1. b   2. a   3. c   4. a

SCANNING FOR DETAILS
1. Vladimir Zworykin; Philo T. Farnsworth
2. glass tubes, electricity; sound, pictures
3. expensive, had problems
4. TV dinners; TV tables
5. information
6. Davy Crockett
7. the American family; way of life
8. two
9. technology
10. computers

ORDERING EVENTS
3, 1, 7, 6, 4, 2, 5

MAKING INFERENCES AND CONCLUDING
1. c   2. b   3. a

UNIT 24

VOCABULARY: MEANING
1. c   2. b   3. b   4. a   5. c   6. a   7. c   8. c   9. a   10. a

USE
Answers will vary.

COMPREHENSION: SKIMMING FOR MAIN IDEAS
1. b   2. b   3. a   4. a

SCANNING FOR DETAILS
1. T   2. T   3. T   4. F   5. F   6. F   7. T
8. F   9. T   10. F

ORDERING EVENTS
6, 5, 3, 4, 2, 7, 1

MAKING INFERENCES AND CONCLUDING
1. b   2. c   3. a